ECONOMIC REFORM IN EUROPE AND THE FORMER SOVIET UNION: IMPLICATIONS FOR INTERNATIONAL FOOD MARKETS

Rod Tyers

Research Report 99
International Food Policy Research Institute
Washington, D.C.

Library of Congress Cataloging-
in-Publication Data

Tyers, Rod.
    Economic reform in Europe and the former
Soviet Union : implications for international food
markets / Rod Tyers.
        p.   cm. — (Research report ; 99)
    Includes bibliographical references.
    ISBN 0-89629-102-2
    1. Food industry and trade—Europe, Eastern.
2. Food industry and trade—Former Soviet republics.
3. Food prices.   4. Europe, Eastern—Economic
policy—1989-   5. Former Soviet republics—
Economic policy. I. International Food Policy Research Institute.   II. Title.   III. Series: Research
report (International Food Policy Research Institute) ; 99.

HD9015.E782T94   1994   94-28850
338.947—dc20   CIP

CONTENTS

TABLES

ILLUSTRATIONS

FOREWORD

As policymakers around the world consider the prognosis for meeting future food needs, among the most difficult factors to forecast are how reforms in Europe and the former Soviet Union countries will affect their agricultural productivity and, in turn, how such changes will affect producers and consumers outside of these regions, especially in the developing world.

Although IFPRI's work largely addresses policies and strategies in developing countries in light of their ability to reduce poverty, hunger, and malnutrition, IFPRI also undertakes work designed to increase understanding of how profound changes in the developed countries affect international trade and hence the developing world. Over the years, IFPRI has looked at issues such as agricultural reforms in the GATT (Research Report 70), the effects of weather and grain yields in the Soviet Union (Research Report 54), and determinants of agricultural policy in the United States and the European Community (Research Report 51).

The research reported here was done by Rod Tyers of the Australian National University while he was a visiting research fellow at IFPRI. The research sheds light on the possible outcomes of economic reforms in Eastern Europe and the former Soviet Union, with a look at how international food markets may change and how developing countries will be affected. Effects of policy changes in Western Europe are also analyzed. While none of us possesses a crystal ball, quantitative analysis such as this provides information on which policymakers can base critical decisions as they prepare to meet the challenges of the next century regarding food, agriculture, and the environment.

Per Pinstrup-Andersen
Director General

ACKNOWLEDGMENTS

The nature of this report necessitated an extensive survey of current research, particularly on the economic reforms in Eastern Europe and the former Soviet Union. Much of that work was not published at the time, and so I am greatly indebted to those who let me see their preliminary results, draft papers, and reports and gave me their time when the advantage to them was slight. In the Economic Research Service of the U.S. Department of Agriculture these include Nancy Cochrane, Bill Coyle, Praveen Dixit, Robert Koopman, Bill Liefert, Mark Lundell, Carl Mabbs-Zeno, Steve Magiera, Vern Roningen, and Jerry Sharples. At the World Bank their number includes Jock Anderson, Antonio Brandao, Karen Brooks, Ed Cook, Max Cordon, Csaba Csaki, John Dixon, Gershon Feder, Alan Gelb, Ian Goldin, Peter Hazell (now at IFPRI) and Will Martin. Karen Brooks was particularly generous with her time in discussions about Soviet agriculture.

On a visit to the Institute for Policy Research, Stan Johnson provided papers and valuable advice. At the Australian Embassy in Washington I was assisted by Agriculture Counsellor John Sault. Kym Anderson, communicating long distance from the GATT, made numerous suggestions and sent recent papers. At Harvard University I received a number of useful comments and suggestions from Peter Rogers, Terry Sicular, and Peter Timmer. At Cambridge I learned a lot about European agriculture from John North. Following a seminar at the University of Birmingham, useful suggestions were made by Henry Scott and Alan Winters. Prue Phillips, of the International Economic Data Bank at the Australian National University, assembled the updated quantity data for the model and assisted in the adaptation of the program to the new data and to operation on a personal computer. Nurul Islam, Romeo Bautista, Yair Mundlak, Dean de Rosa, and Joachim von Braun offered valuable comments at my IFPRI seminars. They and the staff of IFPRI's Trade and Macro-economics Division ensured a pleasant collegial environment during my visit.

Finally, the referees of the draft manuscript have subsequently revealed them-selves to me as Karen Brooks, Nurul Islam, Michiel Keyzer, and Mark Rosegrant. I am grateful to all four for taking the time to study the manuscript and for their insightful comments and suggestions.

1

SUMMARY

As manufacturing relocated to developing countries in recent years, developed-country governments faced intense pressure to generate new employment opportunities. Western Europe sought revitalization through economic integration by expanding membership in the European Community, now the European Union. At the same time, the European Union launched a series of economic reforms that are expected to enhance food consumption but retard production growth. In its effort to rejuvenate its economy, the Soviet Union rejected the system of central planning in favor of a more market-minded economic policy, which eventually destroyed the union and freed the countries of Eastern Europe to choose their own political and economic structures. The results of these changes are expected to have far-reaching effects on all economies, including the developing countries.

This report examines the consequences of the changes that are taking place throughout Europe and the former Soviet Union. Before the dissolution, incentive distortions in agriculture in the Soviet Union favored livestock producers but failed to meet demand on the consumption side. The demand for cereals also rose because grain was used for both direct consumption and animal feed. In the short run, the collapse in aggregate output will reduce purchasing power and hence the demand for livestock products and grain for livestock feed. This change alone, the report finds, could cause a substantial reduction in net food imports.

That the centrally planned economies did a poor job in creating and adopting new technology cannot be disputed, but how much improvement can be expected is hard to determine, given the limitations of past data. For example, management distorted data on production potential for fear that future quotas would be increased if they provided accurate information. Yields in meat were 30-45 percent below those in Western Europe and 20-50 percent below yields in milk. The efficiency of livestock feeding was also poor. Overspending on feedgrains ranged from 75 to 125 percent.

Results suggest that productivity in Eastern Europe could increase by as much as 50 percent for grains and beef and 25 percent for milk production. In the former Soviet Union, grain productivity could increase 10-50 percent; beef, 50 percent; pigmeat, 80 percent; and milk, 100 percent. They could be even higher, considering, first, that prereform supplies of inputs were irregular and unpredictable, and, second, that spoilage rates in storage, transport, and processing were extremely high.

During the reform period, all of the countries in Eastern Europe and the former Soviet Union have suffered severe slumps in output and periods of extremely high inflation. The EE-3 countries—the former Czechoslovakia, Hungary, and Poland—are showing signs of recovery; the Balkan states and former Soviet Union as yet are not.

A search of the literature reveals that one of the most important consequences of economic reforms in Europe and the former Soviet Union is the possible drain on world capital markets, which could possibly mount to US$30-100 billion. One study concludes that if long-term interest rates rise by 1 percentage point, net transfers to the developing countries could be reduced by about US$30 billion a year; another sees real interest rates rising by 3 percentage points, representing a sharp curtailment of net capital flows to developing countries.

Some researchers have concluded that, once the transition to markets and private property is accomplished, the Eastern European countries will do best in export agricultural products and labor-intensive manufactures. With improved technology, the former Soviet Union could have comparative advantage in natural-resource-based goods including agricultural products. However, if booms occur in areas with mineral and energy resources, the growth of food production could be retarded. But the agricultural sector may have the potential to expand more rapidly than other sectors that have received less investment in the past, once farms are broken up into smaller, more efficient sizes. Other studies find, however, that food productivity is likely to remain low until food transport, processing, and marketing systems improve, which will require that improvements in market institutions and infrastructure accompany the move toward more efficient organizational structures.

Three scenarios addressing the effects of the reforms on food demand and supply are considered here. The first is a reference against which the others can be compared. In the second, agriculture recovers slowly, and in the third, general recovery is more prompt. It is assumed that the disruption due to nationalist conflicts will abate and that countries in the region will not return to totalitarian regimes or centrally planned economies. A model, developed earlier on international trade in food commodities and updated and adapted for this report, is fully dynamic in order to examine the path of adjustment to shocks or changes in food policy, but it also estimates the net effects of prices and quantities following full adjustment by farmers and policy-makers. The model only looks at major food staples: wheat, coarse grains, rice, ruminant meats (beef and lamb), nonruminant meats (pigmeat and poultry), dairy products, and sugar.

The anticipated gains under the high-growth scenario are about the same for all foods except dairy products, where the potential in the former Soviet Union seems particularly large. Productivity efficiency in Eastern Europe is expected to improve to the level of Western Europe by 2010, whereas the former Soviet Union is expected to close only half of the gap by that time.

Two changes in the European Union that could have profound effects are incorporated in the simulation: unilateral reforms in the common agricultural policy (CAP) prices and expansion of the European Union to include the countries of the European Free Trade Association. As a result of the reforms, EU production of meat and cereals is reduced and domestic consumption of these products increases. The EU's excess supply declines and world prices rise.

Although the possibility that the EE-3 countries might join the European Union seems unlikely in the near term, steps are being taken to bring their agricultural prices in line with the CAP. Hence the European Union is gradually reducing its barriers against these countries' exports. Although dairy products in the EE-3 countries have the potential to expand sharply, depressing world prices, it seems likely that dairy quotas will be imposed.

In any case, the effects of reforms in the EE-3 countries are likely to be small. Substantial changes therefore depend on changes in the Balkans and the former Soviet Union. In the former Soviet Union, livestock were highly subsidized compared with grains, so liberalization should raise grain production and reduce livestock production (and therefore feedgrain demand). On the consumption side, grain demand for feed and food will be reduced relative to demand for livestock products. Since grain demand will fall and the producer price will rise, a surplus in grain seems inevitable. This result is striking given that the region as a whole has been a net importer of grains for half a century.

Nevertheless, Russia's predicted net grain exports in 2000 still amount to less than a fifth of those predicted for the United States. On average, by the year 2000, the postsocialist countries are expected to be self-sufficient in food, with net export earnings 50-80 percent of those predicted for the United States.

The report also considers the possibility that reforms carried out simultaneously in Western Europe, Eastern Europe, and the former Soviet Union could offset each other and have little effect outside of the region itself. In comparing the original reference simulation with the high-growth scenario for 2000, it is evident that the shift toward excess food supply in the postsocialist economies will have twice the effect on international prices as the shift toward excess demand in Western Europe. The lower international prices resulting from unilateral reforms in Western Europe and the conversion to market economies in Eastern Europe and the former Soviet Union could be on the order of 4-16 percent, most likely between these two extremes. These figures reflect only the effects of reforms in these countries on world prices; reforms brought about in other countries under the agreement on agriculture in the Uruguay Round of the General Agreement on Tariffs and Trade are not considered. However, the tendency of the agreement to make international prices higher will probably be offset by a reduction in discrimination against agricultural sectors in developing countries.

But is a decline in international food prices advantageous for developing countries? Even if all of these countries were net food exporters—which they are not—many might not benefit because their economies are still greatly distorted. To benefit, changes in terms of trade must be transmitted to the domestic market. Many developing countries have insulated their domestic markets from price changes through nontariff barriers or state trading. To complicate matters, the welfare of the poor in rural areas in developing countries depends on the level of economic activity in those areas. The rural poor may be better off with higher food prices if agricultural producer prices are also higher.

Results of an attempt to capture some effects of a food price change on rural economic activity indicate that most developing countries would be marginal net beneficiaries of the decline in world food prices. The exceptions would be Argentina and Thailand, which are substantial net exporters. If developing countries increase their productivity, they could become net food exporters and hence would lose as a result of lower world prices.

2

INTRODUCTION

Shifts of policy regime are not infrequent in many countries. In Europe[1] and the former Soviet Union,[2] however, the period since the mid-1980s has seen extraordinary pressure for economic policy reform. This is due in large part to the rapid decline in the old political order in the former Soviet Union, the associated rebirth of independence in the Eastern or Central European countries, and the reunification of Germany. Also important, however, has been external pressure from Western Europe's trading partners, both directly and through the Uruguay Round of the General Agreement on Tariffs and Trade (GATT), the international trade negotiations originating in 1986. Fundamental to this external pressure has been the increased importance of developing countries in world trade and as exporters of both manufactures and agricultural products. The consequent decline in manufacturing in most industrial countries and their slow overall economic growth has led on the one hand to the search by governments for sources of increased internal efficiency, in the form of deregulation and economic integration, and on the other to conflicting internal pressures for the protection of declining sectors.

In no sector of these economies has this pressure for policy reform been greater than in agriculture. The share of agriculture in gross domestic product (GDP) and total employment has declined more than in manufacturing and for a longer time (Anderson 1987). This decline has nonetheless reduced the cost of collective action by farmers, whose influence over trade policy has been further facilitated by emotional arguments in political fora about the retention of food self-sufficiency and a seemingly idyllic rural lifestyle, one nevertheless forsaken by the great majority of the population. Since the 1940s, Western Europe's farm sector has been increasingly protected. For members of the European Union (EU) this protection has come at least in part from the Common Agricultural Policy (CAP), which retains comparatively high and stable domestic food prices. This fertile policy environment has fostered

---

[1] Western Europe is henceforth taken to include the European Union of 12 (EU-12): Belgium, Denmark, France, Germany, Greece, Ireland, Italy, Luxembourg, the Netherlands, Portugal, Spain, and the United Kingdom. Also included are the countries of the European Free Trade Association (EFTA), Austria, Finland, Iceland, Norway, Sweden, and Switzerland. In most applications, EFTA will refer to the five continental European members of the group. Eastern Europe, which here includes Eastern and Central Europe, comprises the former Czechoslovakia, Hungary, and Poland (the EE-3) and the Balkan states (Albania, Bulgaria, Romania, and the former Yugoslavia). In most applications, EFTA will refer to the five continental European members of the group.

[2] The former Soviet Union includes 15 states: the Baltic states (Estonia, Latvia, and Lithuania), the Russian Federation, the other Western republics (Belarus, Moldova, and Ukraine), the Transcaucasian Federation (Armenia, Azerbaijan, and Georgia), and the Central Asian republics (Kazakhstan, Kyrgyzstan, Tajikistan, Turkmenistan, and Uzbekistan). The former Soviet Union is used rather than the Commonwealth of Independent States because the latter group excludes the Baltic states and Georgia.

substantial improvements in food productivity so that, by the late 1970s, the then European Community had become a net food exporter. Since then the insulation provided by the CAP has required that exports be subsidized, and hence the CAP has changed from a net source of EU government revenue to its largest single expenditure. This change has been the greatest source of pressure for policy reform.

The other, of course, has been from competing food exporters abroad. This group successfully pressed for the inclusion of agricultural protection for discussion in the Uruguay Round of trade negotiations. Their pressure on Western Europe is enhanced by the desirability of other elements of the draft product of those negotiations, namely those covering trade in services and intellectual property rights, which have to date been linked to progress on agriculture (GATT 1991).

Further east, the area encompassing Eastern Europe and the former Soviet Union was, until early this century, a major source of food exports (Anderson 1992). Since then, the decline in the relative size of agriculture's contribution to output and employment has been slower than in Western Europe. As late as 1989, almost a quarter of the Soviet Union's GDP was in agriculture, along with a fifth of its employment (IMF et al. 1991). By comparison, nowhere in Western Europe does agriculture contribute more than 6 percent of GDP (World Bank 1992d).[3] But, while the comparative importance of agriculture in these countries was declining slower, productivity was also falling behind that in Western Europe (Brooks et al. 1991). The net effect was a substantial decline in food self-sufficiency, particularly in the former Soviet Union (Tyers and Anderson 1992, chap.8). This was exacerbated by a decision of the government of the former Soviet Union in the late 1960s to boost consumption (and therefore production) of livestock products and, if necessary, to import feed-grains (Cook 1988).[4]

To add to its problems in agriculture, the other sectors of the Soviet economy grew slowly from the late 1970s. Meanwhile, the Reagan administration in the United States accelerated its arms buildup, placing pressure on the Soviet government to commit still more of the economy's output to defense, even though (current estimates suggest) it had already absorbed almost a quarter of output (Aslund 1991, chap.1). Thus, while governments in Western Europe were casting about for sources of new economic growth, a similar but more urgent search was embarked upon in the Soviet Union. The answer was found in democratization and market-oriented domestic reforms. These would not prove sufficient, however, without a simultaneous scaling down of the military establishment through global arms reduction treaties and withdrawal from Eastern Europe. The latter move led to the practical independence of the Eastern European states, their own democratization, and their programs of economic reform.

The objective of this report is to review the consequences for developing countries of the reforms that are taking place throughout Western and Eastern Europe and the former Soviet Union. In particular, the report examines the region's net trading position in food agriculture, assessing, for example, the conditions under which the region could increase its excess supply of food and hence shift the terms of trade

---

[3]The corresponding proportions for the Eastern European countries are between these two extremes.

[4]And import they did, on a scale that increased dramatically in 1972/73 (Johnson 1975 and 1992, chap.3).

away from food production in developing countries. By reducing agricultural protection, the reforms in Western Europe will restrain future food production growth, but this change is likely to be at least offset by productivity gains in the food sectors of Eastern Europe and the former Soviet Union.

Since the various reforms began, a number of studies have addressed these issues for the region as a whole. A study by the Centre for Economic Policy Research (CEPR) was concerned with the net trading pattern of the postreform Eastern European economies (CEPR 1990). It examines Eastern Europe's factor endowments and finds them high in human capital, suggesting a pattern of comparative advantage that would lead to greatest growth in the exports of sophisticated manufactures intensive in human capital. Its cursory examination of agricultural performance suggests that, despite the probable growth in parts of the manufacturing sector, the potential remains for substantial food productivity increases, leading to expanded net exports of grains.

Hamilton and Winters (1992a, 1992b), who had contributed to the CEPR 1990 study, followed it with a more formal assessment, again just for Eastern European economies. They further examine the evolution of comparative advantage of these countries. Their analysis of skill composition of the labor force finds it on a par with Western Europe. They reexamine the cross-sectional relationship between economic growth and skill level, find it positive, and hence reach optimistic conclusions about the potential for growth in sophisticated manufacturing in Eastern Europe. Of most relevance to this report, however, is their application of a version of the Tyers-Anderson model of world food trade to agricultural production in Eastern Europe. They carry out two experiments. In the first, real household income and food productivity are boosted to represent the net gains from the ongoing economy-wide reforms. Net food exports from Eastern Europe expand and international food prices decline, placing budgetary pressure on the European Union by increasing the net cost of food export subsidies. In the second experiment, they simulate the inclusion of Eastern European farmers in the European Union's CAP and find that the effects on the international market are substantially larger.

Collins and Rodrik (1991) studied the global effects of reform in both Eastern Europe and the former Soviet Union. The first part of their study is focused on possible changes in the direction and composition of trade between Eastern Europe, the former Soviet Union, and the rest of the world. They examine the pattern of output per worker in agriculture and manufacturing and estimate revealed comparative advantage from prereform trade flows. They also examine the possibility of net food exports, though they are skeptical of the CEPR result that manufacturing growth will be at the capital-intensive end. This, they say, depends on substantial capital inflows, which seem slow in coming.[5] Collins and Rodrik are also concerned with the potential effects on global interest rates of a substantial inflow of capital to Eastern Europe and the former Soviet Union. These effects, which are discussed in Chapter 4 of this report, are likely to be of more significance for developing countries than the inevitable shifts in the terms of merchandise (including food) trade examined by the CEPR and Hamilton and Winters.

---

[5]There is now evidence that these flows are appearing, particularly in Hungary (IMF 1992a).

A more recent study by Overbosch and Tims (1992) focuses on the food trade consequences of the Eastern Europe and former Soviet Union reforms. They apply the basic linked system of national models developed at the International Institute for Applied Systems Analysis to three reform scenarios. No model of the Eastern Europe or former Soviet Union economies is incorporated. Rather, these scenarios are built on prereform external trade data for that region, modified according to assumptions about the (internal versus external) direction of that trade. Nevertheless, their results also show the potential for substantial increases in the region's excess food supply and for lower relative food prices in the medium term. Finally, Liefert, Cook, and Koopman (1989), Liefert, Koopman, and Cook (1991), and Koopman (1992) report U.S. Department of Agriculture (USDA) analysis of incentive distortions in the former Soviet Union using the SWOPSIM model. This is the only work that examines these distortions, and it highlights the tendency of Soviet policy to discriminate against cereal production and in favor of the livestock industry.

Finally, substantial research on the economies of Eastern Europe and the former Soviet Union, particularly their agricultural sectors, has been done recently at the World Bank.[6] These studies emphasize developments in the current transitional stage of the reforms. For example, while the studies recognize the potential for substantial improvements in food productivity in the former Soviet Union economy, they emphasize the World Bank's agenda for further reforms and associated investments, deeming that these reforms must be successfully completed before improvements can be realized. Nevertheless, they are optimistic about the overall economy of the former Soviet Union, to the extent that aggregate output and consumption are projected to bottom out in 1993 and 1994 and recover thereafter. In the food sector, they conclude that domestic price reform will lead to an increased commitment of resources to grain production and less to the presently inefficient livestock industry.

This report draws on these and other studies. Its scope is narrower than many in that it emphasizes behavioral responses in the food sector only, but it encompasses reforms in both Western and Eastern Europe and the former Soviet Union. Chapter 3 reviews the evidence on internal incentive distortions and comparative food productivity in Eastern Europe and the former Soviet Union, while Chapter 4 briefly summarizes recent developments as well as some transitional consequences of the reforms for the developing countries. In Chapter 5 a newly updated version of the original Tyers-Anderson model of world trade in food products is used to estimate the effects of reforms in Western Europe, Eastern Europe, and the former Soviet Union. Four possible scenarios are examined. Estimates of each region's domestic incentive distortions are incorporated explicitly in the model, and the consequences of reforms are quantified over a 20-year horizon. Chapter 6 summarizes the implications for developing countries, and Chapter 7 presents the conclusions.

---

[6]For the work on the economy of the former Soviet Union, see World Bank 1992a, chap.12; 1992b. These reports were released at the September 1992 meeting of the World Bank Board.

3

THE PREREFORM ECONOMIES

The region studied in this report, comprising all of Europe and the former Soviet Union, has a sixth of the world's population and generates fully a third of its recorded output.[7] Changes of policy regime there cannot but have a substantial impact on the economy of the rest of the world. Throughout this report, the region is disaggregated into five major subregions (Table 1). The former Soviet Union is further subdivided into six groups of new republics, the constituents of which are also listed. The inaccuracy of GDP as a measure of development notwithstanding, it is immediately clear from the table that the region as a whole is very heterogeneous in the levels of development achieved.[8] All of the former Soviet Union is in the World Bank's lower-middle income category, with its Central Asian republics at the bottom end of that range. Eastern Europe and the former Soviet Union together have more than half the population of the region as a whole, but little more than a tenth of the income.

Consistent with this heterogeneity is the economic contribution of agriculture in the region. While agriculture supplies less than 6 percent of the output in all the constituent countries of the European Union and the European Free Trade Association (EFTA), it contributes an average of about 14 percent in Eastern Europe and almost 25 percent in the former Soviet Union.[9] Moreover, much of the former Soviet Union has retained between 20 and 40 percent of its labor force in agriculture, compared with an average for Western Europe of less than 7 percent (IMF 1992c, Table 9). Accordingly, differences are to be expected in the patterns of food consumption between the poor and the wealthy parts of the region. These are observed, although the differences are not as pronounced as the apparent income disparities

---

[7]The numerators in these fractions appear in Table 1, while the denominators are the world totals provided in the World Development Indicators section of World Bank 1992d, Tables 1 and 3.

[8]No attempt has been made here to use International Comparison Project methods or to otherwise adjust for purchasing power parity. Note, however, that the estimates by Summers and Heston (1991) of 1985 per capita GNP for the Eastern European and former Soviet Union economies (expressed in 1980 US dollars) were: Czechoslovakia, US$7,400; Hungary, US$5,800; Poland, US$4,900; Bulgaria, US$5,100; Romania, US$4,300; Yugoslavia, US$5,100; and the Soviet Union, US$6,300. Considering that 1980 US dollars are more valuable than 1990 ones by about half, these prereform estimates are larger than those in Table 1 by factors of four or more. More recent evidence on purchasing power parity suggests a ratio of three or less (Konovalov et al. 1993, *Economist* 1993a). There are several reasons for discrepancies between these sources: new accounting information has become available since these economies opened formally, output in each has slumped as reforms have begun, and the price indices used by Summers and Heston to adjust for purchasing power parity probably omitted substantial hidden inflation.

[9]See World Bank 1992d, World Development Indicators, Table 3, and IMF et al. (1991), vol.1, Table A.5.

Table 1—Gross domestic product (GDP) and population in Europe and the former Soviet Union, about 1990

Economic Group/ Country	GDP	Percent of Total	Population	Percent of Total	Average GDP per Capita	Percent of European Union
	(US$ billion)		(millions)		(US$)	
EU-12[a]	5,420	77.0	326	42.0	16,600	100
EFTA-5[b]	860	12.0	34	4.0	25,300	152
EE-3	142	2.0	65	8.0	2,200	13
Former Czechoslovakia	45	0.6	16	2.0	2,800	17
Hungary	33	0.5	11	1.0	3,000	18
Poland	64	0.9	38	5.0	1,700	10
Balkans	142	2.0	59	8.0	2,400	14
Albania	5	. . .	3	0.4	1,500	9
Bulgaria	20	0.3	9	1.0	2,200	13
Romania	35	0.5	23	3.0	1,500	9
Former Yugoslavia	82	1.0	24	3.0	3,400	21
Former Soviet Union	490	7.0	289	38.0	1,700	10
Russia	300	4.0	148	19.0	2,000	12
Ukraine	79	1.0	52	7.0	1,500	9
Baltic states	15	0.2	9	1.0	1,900	11
Estonia	3	. . .	2	0.2	1,840	11
Latvia	5	. . .	3	0.3	2,000	12
Lithuania	7	. . .	4	0.5	1,900	11
Western republics	47	0.7	30	4.0	1,600	9
Armenia	4	. . .	3	0.4	1,300	8
Azerbaijan	8	0.1	7	0.9	1,200	7
Belarus	21	0.3	10	1.0	2,000	12
Georgia	8	0.1	6	0.7	1,400	9
Moldova	6	. . .	4	0.6	1,300	8
Kazakhstan	21	0.3	17	2.0	1,300	8
Central Asia	28	0.4	33	5.0	800	5
Kyrgyzstan	4	. . .	4	0.6	900	5
Tajikistan	4	. . .	5	0.7	800	5
Turkmenistan	4	. . .	4	0.5	1,100	7
Uzbekistan	16	0.2	20	3.0	800	5
Total or average	7,054	100.0	773	100.0	9,700	58

Sources: For the EU-12, EFTA-5 and EE-3, all estimates are from the World Development Indicators supplement of World Bank, *World Development Report 1992* (New York: Oxford University Press, 1992), Tables 1 and 3. For the former U.S.S.R., GDP is based on shares from IMF (International Monetary Fund), *World Economic Outlook* (Washington, D.C.: IMF, 1992), Table 9, combined with the 1990 GDP estimate of R 622 billion from IMF, *The Russian Federation*, Economic Review Series (Washington, D.C.: IMF, 1992) converted to US$ at the exchange rate R 1.27 per US$1.00. The latter rate is that used in comparison analysis by the International Economics Department of the World Bank, *Measuring the Incomes of Economies of the Former Soviet Union*, WPS 1057 (Washington, D.C.: World Bank, 1992).

Notes: Values for the centrally planned economies are generally given only to two significant figures of accuracy. Numbers may not add to totals due to rounding. The ellipses (. . .) indicate less than 0.1 percent.

[a]EU-12 includes the 12 countries belonging to the European Union: Belgium, Denmark, France, Germany, Greece, Ireland, Italy, Luxembourg, the Netherlands, Portugal, Spain, and the United Kingdom.

[b]EFTA-5 includes the continental members of the European Free Trade Association: Austria, Finland, Norway, Sweden, and Switzerland. Iceland is excluded.

might suggest (Table 2). In general, the world's developing countries directly consume much more grain and fewer livestock products than do the industrial ones. Characteristically, then, the patterns of food consumption in Eastern Europe and the former Soviet Union lie between those in Western Europe and all other developing countries. But, even in the poorer part of the former Soviet Union, the share of food expenditure on dairy products remains on a par with the European Union. Of course this does not mean that the volume consumed per capita is the same. In the late 1980s milk intake was about 170 kilograms per capita, still below the 208 kilograms per capita consumed in the industrial countries (OECD 1991, 177). Meat consumption was 59 kilograms per capita, compared with 84 kilograms per capita in the industrial countries. Nevertheless, for countries that are comparatively poor, these levels of consumption are high.

Sedik (1992) explains this as a consequence of a deliberate policy throughout Eastern Europe and the former Soviet Union to raise livestock product consumption, beginning in the 1960s. In his view, the goal was achieved by heavily subsidizing the livestock sector. But it is now known that the region's consumption of these products was already high for its level of development, even in the 1960s (OECD 1991). More likely, people in Eastern Europe and the former Soviet Union are predisposed toward herding, and therefore their diets are rich in animal proteins, at least compared with much of the developing world. For example, large parts of South and East Asia have cultural inhibitions that limit the consumption of meat, particularly meat from cattle. Indeed, there is evidence (to be discussed later) that the incentive prices for livestock products in the former Soviet Union were high by international standards.

Table 2—Expenditure shares on food products, 1990

GLS Product[a]	EU-12	EFTA-5	EE-3	Balkans	Russia	Rest of Former Soviet Union	All Developing Countries
				(percent)			
Grains	11	9	14	26	15	20	47
Rice	1	1	0	1	1	1	26
Wheat	7	5	10	19	9	15	11
Coarse grain	3	3	4	6	5	4	10
Sugar	5	4	4	3	4	4	6
Dairy products	31	43	34	24	34	31	14
Meats	53	45	48	47	47	41	33
Ruminant	23	21	15	17	30	26	18
Nonruminant	30	24	33	30	17	15	15
Total	100	100	100	100	100	100	100

Source: Benchmark trend consumption estimates are from the updated Tyers-Anderson model database, detailed in Appendix 2, and described in R. Tyers and K. Anderson, *Disarray in World Food Markets: A Quantitative Assessment* (Cambridge, U.K.: Cambridge University Press, 1992).

Note: Numbers may not add to totals due to rounding. EU-12 is the European Union of 12 countries. EFTA-5 includes the continental members of the European Free Trade Association: Austria, Finalnd, Norway, Sweden, and Switzerland. The EE-3 countries are the former Czechoslovakia, Hungary, and Poland. The Balkans include Albania, Bulgaria, Romania, and the former Yugoslavia.

[a]GLS refers to grains, livestock products, and sugar, the food groups of interest in this report.

Producer and Consumer Incentive Distortions

Since the 1950s in Western Europe, the decline in agriculture's contributions to GDP and employment has mirrored the decline in the share of overall household income committed to food products. The number of farm households has also declined in absolute terms, reducing the free-rider cost of collective action by farmers. At the same time, agriculture's comparative smallness and the lower share of income spent on food have reduced the proportional direct and indirect tax burdens associated with assistance to agriculture. These changes, combined with the emotive force of the arguments for food self-sufficiency and the preservation of traditional rural lifestyles, have yielded increasingly high rates of protection to agriculture relative to other tradable goods sectors.[10] This trend is confirmed by the changes in agricultural prices relative to prices of other tradable goods since the early 1960s (Table 3). Despite the persistent declining trend of agricultural prices in international trade, relative agricultural prices have remained high in Western Europe. This pattern appears not only in the European Union, where the CAP has been notorious for its protectionism, but it is even more pronounced in the Western European countries whose agricultural policies have been independent of the CAP.

A modern measure of assistance to agriculture, which can be hidden in a number of ways, is the producer subsidy equivalent (PSE). This measure consolidates all assistance into an equivalent specific subsidy payment, which is readily expressed as an equivalent ad valorem product price distortion such as an equivalent tariff or

Table 3—Indices of agricultural prices relative to industrial prices in Western Europe and in international markets

Period	EC-10[a] Prices (1)	EFTA-5[b] Prices (2)	International Prices (3)	EC-10[a] International Prices (4)	EFTA-5[b] International Prices (5)
			(1961-64 = 100)		
1961-64	100	100	100	1.00	1.00
1965-69	101	105	99	1.02	1.06
1970-74	99	104	100	0.99	1.04
1975-79	106	102	89	1.19	1.15
1980-84	97	114	83	1.17	1.37
1985-87	90	98	70	1.29	1.40

Source: R. Tyers and K. Anderson, *Disarray in World Food Markets: A Quantitative Assessment* (Cambridge, U.K.: Cambridge University Press, 1992), Table 2.1.

Notes: The first two columns show the prices received by farmers relative to the prices received by producers of other tradable goods (as reflected in the wholesale price index). The third column shows an index of agricultural prices relative to manufactured export prices for all industrial market economies.

[a]EC-10 excludes Portugal and Spain from the European Union countries.

[b]EFTA-5 includes the continental members of the European Free Trade Association: Austria, Finland, Norway, Sweden, and Switzerland.

---

[10]For a more detailed discussion of the determinants of increased agricultural protection, see Tyers and Anderson 1992, chap.3.

export subsidy.[11] Its major weakness is that it is not a good measure of the impact of protection on international trade, mainly because some forms of assistance to farmers are "decoupled" (so that the assistance does not affect production incentives at the margin) and others are associated with controls on the use of land (Hertel 1989; Roningen and Dixit 1991). Thus, its use in the analysis of trade effects of protection requires that associated quantitative controls be examined explicitly. The PSE and the corresponding measure of consumer price distortions, the consumer subsidy equivalent (CSE), are now estimated annually for the industrial countries by OECD (1992). For other countries, including those of Eastern Europe and the former Soviet Union, these measures are estimated periodically by the Economic Research Service of the USDA (Webb, Lopez, and Penn 1990; Cook, Liefert, and Koopman 1991).

For this report, estimates of PSEs and CSEs for 1989 and 1990 have been drawn from these sources, converted into ad valorem product price subsidies, and expressed as nominal protection coefficients (equivalent domestic-to-border price ratios). The results are listed in Table 4. Those for the EFTA group are highest, consistent with that group's comparatively high incomes and comparatively small agricultural sectors. Producer incentive distortions are uniformly greater than those facing consumers, reflecting the use of assistance measures that do not distort the product price directly. By comparing the EFTA distortions with those in the European Union, it is clear that expansion of the European Union to include the EFTA countries, and hence the extension of the CAP to EFTA farmers, will reduce the overall level of assistance to food production in Western Europe.

Beginning with these measures, the estimation of the trade effects of Western Europe's distortions is a comparatively simple application of partial equilibrium analysis, provided quantity controls are properly accounted for. This is because the agricultural sector is small, there are no associated exchange controls, and other tradable goods sectors are only lightly protected. It is no longer convenient to estimate distortions in Eastern Europe and the former Soviet Union, however. These economies not only used multiple controlled exchange rates in the prereform period but, in all sectors, most quantity decisions were dictated centrally and official prices were set to satisfy distributional objectives rather than to ration supply. In the former Soviet Union, for example, the net effect appears to have been a trade regime that discriminated heavily against natural resource-based exports, particularly oil and gas, and subsidized imports of staple foods and some industrial inputs (Konovalov et al. 1993).

While it remains possible to estimate PSEs and CSEs for agriculture in Eastern Europe and the former Soviet Union, the resulting estimates are particularly sensitive to the method by which product and input prices are calculated. Since quoted prices do not generally direct the choice of production or consumption volumes, adjustments are required. The adjusted prices, then, are compared against a set of border

---

[11]First suggested in Josling 1973, the PSE is calculated by commodity and evaluated as a sum of money representing the total value of transfers received by producers of that commodity. This can be compared with the total value of the product measured at free market prices (usually border prices adjusted for infrastructural costs). It can be expressed either as the difference of the two values or the proportion by which the distorted value differs from the free market value. For a more complete explanation, see Tangermann, Josling, and Pearson 1987.

Table 4—**Food price distortions in Europe and the former Soviet Union expressed as the ratio of the equivalent domestic incentive price to the border price**

Economic Group	Rice	Wheat	Coarse Grain	Sugar	Dairy Products	Ruminant Meat	Non-ruminant Meat	All GLS[a]
European Union								
Producer	2.78	1.75	2.22	2.27	4.00	2.33	1.54	2.52
Consumer	2.33	1.54	1.89	1.92	2.50	1.89	1.33	1.88
EFTA-5[b]								
Producer	1.00	8.33	4.00	3.33	6.67	3.70	2.78	4.97
Consumer	1.00	2.22	2.56	2.38	2.78	2.63	2.33	2.57
EE-3								
Producer	0.90	1.08	1.22	0.76	0.84	1.67	1.08	1.10
Consumer	0.90	0.88	1.22	1.13	0.46	0.80	0.98	0.83
Balkans[c]								
Producer	1.00	0.87	1.00	0.47	1.00	0.91	0.83	0.91
Consumer	1.00	0.87	1.00	0.47	1.00	0.91	0.83	0.91
Former Soviet Union								
Producer	1.82	0.63	0.73	1.30	1.55	1.11	1.11	1.79
Consumer	0.34	0.22	0.35	0.84	0.52	0.54	0.99	0.80
Average for Eastern Europe and the former Soviet Union								
Producer	1.77	0.73	0.86	1.10	1.30	1.16	1.05	1.10
Consumer	0.43	0.40	0.46	0.84	0.56	0.59	0.96	0.62

Sources: Based on estimates of producer subsidy equivalents (PSEs) and consumer subsidy equivalents (CSEs) for Western Europe in 1990 provided by the Organization for Economic Cooperation and Development (OECD) on computer diskette to supplement *Agricultural Policies, Markets, and Trade: Monitoring and Outlook 1992* (Paris: OECD, 1992) and for Eastern Europe and the former Soviet Union as provided by the Europe Branch of the Economic Research Service of the U.S. Department of Agriculture (USDA). The origins of the former Soviet Union estimates are detailed in Table 6.

Notes: Incentive distortions are here expressed as equivalent nominal protection coefficients (NPCs, or ratios of domestic to border prices) adjusted to also represent (as equivalent product price effects) those input price distortions accounted for in the calculation of PSEs and CSEs by the OECD and the USDA, Economic Research Service.

There is a one-to-one relationship between NPCs and PSEs and CSEs. For the PSE (expressed as a proportion of payments to producers), π^p, the equivalent NPC is $\rho^p = 1/(1-\pi^p)$. For the corresponding CSE, π^c, it is $\rho^c = 1/(1+\pi^c)$.

Since the estimates in this table are essential to the analysis in Chapter 5, it is completed by assumption even where the supporting information is incomplete. To achieve this, consumer distortions are assumed to be the same as producer distortions in the Balkan states, and the nonexistence in many cases of estimates of PSEs or CSEs for rice is taken to indicate a free market.

[a]GLS refers to grains, livestock products, and sugar, the food groups of interest in this report.
[b]EFTA-5 includes the continental members of the European Free Trade Association: Austria, Finland, Norway, Sweden, and Switzerland.
[c] Both PSE and CSE estimates for Hungary and all the Balkan states are not available. The estimates used are PSEs and the Balkan estimates are for Yugoslavia only in 1988.

prices, converted to domestic currency at, most properly, the (equilibrium) exchange rate that would apply in the absence of exchange controls and distortions elsewhere in the economy.

Considering first the choice of prices, on the demand side, in the prereform former Soviet Union, there was excess demand for sugar and livestock products at the heavily subsidized prereform state shop prices; only some citizens could obtain these products (usually via their employers) without spending many hours queuing. Consumers would clearly have been prepared to pay higher (incentive) prices for these commodities if they could have obtained them without wasting time in queues. This view follows Becker's (1965) theory of the allocation of time in its recent application to centrally planned economies (Stahl and Alexeev 1985). In this literature, incentive, "virtual," and "effort" prices are overlapping concepts.[12] There are two approaches to their estimation. Liefert (1991) relies on the assumption that planners are aware of the excess demand at state shop prices and that they control it at a roughly constant level by manipulating the level of imports. Koopman (1992) applies this approach to the adjustment of CSE estimates. His adjustments remain in the coefficients for the EE-3 (the former Czechoslovakia, Hungary, and Poland) and the Balkan states in Table 4.

Given the coexistence of state shops with private food markets, called *kolkhoz*, in most of the former socialist countries, a more appealing approach relies on data from these "parallel markets." Charemza (1990) proposes the use of data on parallel markets to estimate demand parameters, which can then be applied in the calculations of excess demand at state prices. For the former Soviet Union, Morduch, Brooks, and Urinson (1994) adopt a related approach. They reason that, where like products are available in both state shops and private markets, the consumer of the marginal unit is indifferent as to whether the purchase is made at the low state shop price, with its associated queue, or at the higher private market price. The private market prices are therefore estimates of incentive prices.[13] Their data, which are summarized in Table 5, are derived from Russia's Goskomstat consumption and price statistics and unpublished household budget surveys in 1991. They show that the private markets for meat, milk, and eggs are heavily patronized, supplying about a fifth of total consumption (most of which, of course, is purchased by higher-income households). Moreover, the incentive price premia are quite large. Meats and dairy products increase threefold and sugar doubles. Anecdotal evidence suggests that these premia were lower before the reforms began to take effect, more so for dairy products than for meats. Accordingly, the consumption coefficients for the former Soviet Union in Table 4 are adjusted upward in Table 6.

Morduch, Brooks, and Urinson (1994) suggest that not all state shop consumers waste time queuing and that consumption rents accrue. Indeed, they make the extreme assumption that none of this rent is wasted. Consumption is then modeled as a purchase at the estimated incentive price, combined with an associated inframarginal consumer subsidy (a transfer to consumers that does not induce them to change their level of consumption, given the incentive price). Their point is that price liberalization, while it removes the queues, also removes the inframarginal subsidy, leaving poorer groups considerably worse off. For the poorest households, 13 percent of the sample of 1991 households, they reason that full compensation for

---

[12]While it will be convenient here to treat the calculus of these prices as identical with that of market prices, there are important differences. First and most obvious, the whole incentive price paid is not received by the supplier of the good purchased, some disappearing in queuing or search waste. Indeed, Boycko (1992) builds a macroeconomic model on microeconomic foundations that includes queuing waste, which helps to explain some of the former Soviet Union's observed loss of output in the early reform period. Second, the incentive price for a particular good is not the same for all consumers, most often because of differences in the opportunity cost of queuing time (Sah 1987).

[13]This reasoning follows that in earlier studies of Chinese food policies. See Sicular (1989; 1991).

Table 5—Food consumption and prices on state and private markets in the former Soviet Union

Item	Meat	Milk[a]	Eggs[a]	Sugar	Potatoes	Vegetables	Fruit
Average annual consumption per person[a]	(kilograms/capita)						
State shops and cooperatives	53	278	166	25	64	61	27
Kolkhoz (free) markets	12	61	37	0	17	19	9
	(percent)						
Share from free markets	19	18	18	0	21	23	24
Consumer prices	(rubles)						
State shops	7.0	0.65	0.26	2.4	1.0	1.0	3.0
Cooperatives	14.0	0.65	0.27	3.5	1.5	4.0	6.0
Kolkhoz (free) markets	25.0	1.95	0.67	5.0	1.5	5.0	12.0

Source: Averages from disaggregated data collected in 1991, presented in the appendix to J. Morduch, K. Brooks, and Y.M. Urinson, "Distributional Consequences of the Russian Price Liberalization," *Economic Development and Cultural Change* 4 (3, 1994): 469-483.

[a]Volumes are in kilograms except for milk, which is in liters, and eggs, which are in numbers of eggs.

Table 6—Assumptions about prereform price distortions in the former Soviet Union

Price Distortions	Rice	Wheat	Coarse Grain	Sugar	Dairy Products	Ruminant Meat	Non-ruminant Meat
Consumer price distortions							
From CSE estimates	0.50	0.33	0.52	0.96	0.52	0.40	0.74
Assumed incentive ratio	1.00	1.00	1.00	1.30	1.50	2.00	2.00
Assumed overvaluation factor[a]	0.67	0.67	0.67	0.67	0.67	0.67	0.67
Estimates used	0.34	0.22	0.35	0.84	0.52	0.54	0.99
Producer price distortions[b]							
From PSE estimates	1.82	0.63	0.73	1.30	1.55	1.11	1.11
Factor for excluded subsidies	1.50	1.50	1.50	1.50	1.50	1.50	1.50
Assumed overvaluation factor[a]	0.67	0.67	0.67	0.67	0.67	0.67	0.67
Estimates used	1.82	0.63	0.73	1.30	1.55	1.11	1.11

Sources: Based on estimates of producer subsidy equivalents (PSEs) and consumer subsidy equivalents (CSEs) for the former Soviet Union as provided by the Economic Research Service, the U.S. Department of Agriculture. Although they are updated to 1989, the method used in estimating them and the policy instruments included and excluded are detailed in E. Cook, W.M. Liefert, and R. Koopman, "Government Intervention in Soviet Agriculture: Estimates of Consumer and Producer Subsidy Equivalents," Staff Report No. AGES 9146, U.S. Department of Agriculture, Economic Research Service, Washington, D.C., 1991; and R. B. Koopman, "Agriculture's Role During the Transition from Plan to Market: Real Prices, Real Incentives and Potential Equilibrium," paper prepared for a conference on Economic Statistics for the Economies in Transition: Eastern Europe in the 1990s, U.S. Department of Agriculture, Washington, D.C., 1992.

Notes: Incentive distortions are here expressed as equivalent nominal protection coefficients (NPCs, or ratios of domestic to border prices) adjusted to also represent (as equivalent product price effects) those input price distortions accounted for in the calculation of PSEs and CSEs by the Economic Research Service. There is a one-to-one relationship between these and PSEs and CSEs. For the PSE (expressed as a proportion of payments to producers), π^p, the equivalent NPC is $\rho^p = 1/(1-\pi^p)$. For the corresponding CSE, π^c, it is $\rho^c = 1/(1+\pi^c)$.

[a]Exchange controls and other distortions not accounted for in the PSE and CSE calculations are assumed to have reduced the relative prices of food products by a third.

[b]It is assumed that state and collective farms in the former Soviet Union produced both cereals and livestock products and that the opportunity cost of cereal sales for direct consumption is the producer price, rather than the more heavily subsidized consumer price.

this change would require a doubling of wage income. For an average household, the reduction in purchasing power would be 39 percent (Morduch, Brooks, and Urinson 1994, Table 2).

That there was no queuing waste in the prereform former Soviet Union is a strong assumption. Moskoff's (1984) description of the Soviet labor market suggests that overtime payments, part-time work, and holding of two jobs were common. Indeed, McAuley (1979, 248) finds that, in the 1970s, incentive and supplementary payments were 40 percent of the average worker's wage. Even though many senior bureaucrats, the military, and others with private links to the food industry would have made their purchases without queuing, it is more likely that most of the inframarginal consumer subsidy was wasted (as argued, for example, in Boycko 1992 and Tarr 1991). Accordingly, in the analysis in Chapter 5, price liberalization is not accompanied by any related reduction in household disposable income. A less satisfactory analysis in which an intermediate assumption is made is presented in Tyers 1993.

On the supply side, since profit-maximizing firms would generally not choose the observed output when confronted by the observed prices, the appropriate prices to use are those at which profit-maximizing firms would choose the observed output. Planners can coerce firms to produce more than the profit-maximizing output while still covering average costs. The (incentive) price at which competitive firms would produce that output is therefore higher, as explained by Koopman (1992) and Liefert, Koopman, and Cook (1991). Koopman's supply disequilibrium adjustments are incorporated into the PSEs on which Table 4 is based.

Also important as distortions of production incentives are a number of subsidies that were omitted from the PSE estimates due to lack of sufficiently detailed information. In particular, state farm debts were routinely written off by the Central Bank in the 1980s. Anecdotal evidence suggests that these debts grew rapidly in the latter part of that decade and that, by its end, revenue on many state farms fell so low that they could not cover recurrent material costs.[14] Indirect subsidies of this magnitude are too important to ignore, even if allowance for them must be arbitrary. Accordingly, on the assumption that subsidies in this form were not biased toward particular food products, all the former Soviet Union producer coefficients were arbitrarily raised by 50 percent, as indicated in Table 6.

Next the choice of exchange rate is considered. No truly robust estimates of equilibrium exchange rates appear to exist for the prereform period. One could try the method recently applied to developing countries with exchange controls (Bautista 1987; Krueger, Schiff, and Valdés 1988; Dorosh and Valdés 1990). But this approach requires that the distortions in the economy can be estimated from product price comparisons or at least that some unsustainable component of the current account imbalance can be identified, and that economy-wide behavioral elasticities with which to calculate the degree of overvaluation are available. Such methods are virtually impossible to use when few domestic prices clear their respective markets. The gargantuan task of correcting for disequilibria in all tradable product markets must first be completed.

---

[14]Personal communication, Ed Cook, Commonwealth of Independent States Department, World Bank, September 1992.

In their estimates for the former Soviet Union, for example, Cook, Liefert, and Koopman (1991) judge the official rate to be overvalued almost threefold. To arrive at this, they use Liefert's (1990) shadow (rather than equilibrium) exchange rate estimates. Liefert evaluates the domestic resource cost in rubles of displacing one dollar's worth of imports in the marginal industry—that industry in which the former Soviet Union had the greatest comparative disadvantage.[15] The result is an average rate for the period 1985-87 of R 1.90 per US$1.00. The corresponding official rate in 1986 was R 0.70. In his subsequent analysis of agricultural incentive distortions in 1989, Koopman (1992) assumes about the same degree of overvaluation for the former Soviet Union and, in the Eastern European economies, overvaluation by about a third. Koopman's results for 1989 are the primary source for the PSE and CSE estimates in Table 6.[16] Because more recent evidence from the former Soviet Union indicates that a larger real devaluation is likely to be sustained, however, a more substantial overvaluation of the prereform ruble is assumed in Table 6.[17] No additional overvaluation is incorporated in the Table 4 estimates for Eastern Europe. With the exception of Poland, there has not been a consistent pattern of large real devaluations in Eastern Europe. And since 1989, the trend throughout appears to have been toward real revaluations.[18]

The many arbitrary assumptions made in the construction of the Eastern Europe and former Soviet Union entries in Table 4 imply that any analysis that uses these results as a starting point should be interpreted cautiously. One should bear in mind, however, that many of these estimates remain robust. Most particularly, the relativities across individual food markets stem from careful examination of observable instruments by the USDA's Economic Research Service and from observations of average state shop and private market retail prices. The arbitrariness applies to distortions affecting the food sector in its entirety so that all the estimates for Eastern Europe and the former Soviet Union in Table 4, or all of the food production data for grains, livestock products, and sugar (GLS), are simultaneously raised or lowered, which in turn would raise or lower all of the producer incentive distortions. These arbitrary adjustments are examined in a sensitivity analysis presented in Chapter 5.

---

[15]Liefert chooses agriculture as that marginal import-competing industry.

[16]Much of the information for these estimates was assembled by Ed Cook (prior to his departure to the World Bank), Nancy Cochrane, and Mark Lundell of the Economic Research Service, USDA.

[17]Central Bank auctions in Russia (participation in which was restricted to just a few institutions) yielded a rate of R 9.50 per US$1.00 as early as 1989 (IMF 1992b). By 1990, the Central Bank auction rate had risen to about 20, while black markets in Moscow and Vienna were trading at 16 (IMF et al. 1991). This suggests that, at R 0.6 per US$1.00, the official rate in that year was more overvalued than previously and that Koopman's 1989 estimates (in the form of the NPCs of Table 4) are biased upward. This view is further supported by the substantial real devaluation that occurred in 1991 after the ruble was floated. In 1991, for example, while nominal consumer prices doubled, the nominal ruble per dollar rate rose more than 30-fold. Since then, however, it appears that price increases have been catching up (IMF 1992b) and, indeed, the real value of the ruble appears to have stabilized in early 1993.

[18]See Coricelli and Rocha (1991) and, for more recent evidence, IMF 1992a. The latter shows that real effective rates in the EE-3 did fall temporarily but have since recovered all of the lost ground in Czechoslovakia and Hungary. In Poland the real effective rate index remains lower than that in 1985 by 28 percent. It reached its lowest point, however, in 1990 and has increased since. The data from which corresponding trends in the Balkans might be observed are incomplete. Calculations by PlanEcon (1992) suggest real revaluations from early 1990 in most Eastern European countries.

The Potential for Food Productivity Improvements

There is little dispute that the centrally planned economies have performed poorly in the creation and adoption of new technology and, for this reason and others, in the overall efficiency with which the available resources have been exploited (Bergson 1991). What remains unclear is whether the difference in performance can be explained simply by the absence of unfettered private markets and private profit-maximizing firms. If this were true, the obvious information limitations associated with central planning, combined with distorted management incentives (the hiding of production potential, for example, for fear of increased future quotas), should engender both allocative inefficiency across industries and technical inefficiency at the level of the enterprise. Murrell (1991b) reviews a number of recent studies that compare technical and allocative efficiency in Eastern Europe and the former Soviet Union with that in industrial market economies. Although these are conducted with difficulty, given the poor comparability of statistics, the results do not identify any consistent pattern of inferiority in the centrally planned economies. Koopman (1989), for example, allows for differences in technology between market and centrally planned economies and finds that average *technical* inefficiency in Soviet agriculture during 1960-79 was not greatly different from that in a number of industrial market economies, including the United States. What does differ between the market and centrally planned economies is the "best practice" level of productivity used as the standard in each case. The rate of innovation within enterprises and the rate of inward diffusion of technology in the centrally planned economies have been uncommonly low and their technology has become increasingly backward.

The freeing up of trade in both goods and information between Eastern Europe, the former Soviet Union, and the rest of the world should facilitate a period of catching up, during which food productivity could increase substantially. A number of recent studies have attempted to gauge the extent of technical backwardness in the food sector, and thence the potential for productivity improvements, by comparing average yields. Although the comparatively poor performance of the Eastern European and former Soviet Union food sectors is evident from such comparisons, they are fraught with dangers of aggregation bias and incomplete information about production conditions. Recent examples include Cook 1988, Figures 1-3; OECD 1991, Table 50; World Bank 1992c, Box 12-1, and 1992b, especially Tables 2.5 and 2.10; and Koopman 1992, Table 5. The comparisons are of crop yields, livestock productivity (meat, milk, and egg yields per animal), and feeding efficiency (feed weight per unit of meat, milk, or eggs produced).

To begin with the grain sector, average yields in Eastern Europe were only slightly lower than those in Western Europe in the presocialist period (1925-33), according to Koopman.[19] The average yield of wheat in Poland, for example, was on a par with its counterpart in Western Europe, although that for barley was slightly below it. Since then, however, Polish yields have fallen well behind those in the

---

[19]This is ongoing work in the Europe branch of the Economic Research Service, USDA. A brief summary of the former Soviet Union part of this work is provided in Koopman (1992).

West. Both are now only two-thirds of the average yield achieved across all of Western Europe. In the former Soviet Union, where growing conditions for grains are not as consistently productive as those in Western and Central Europe, wheat and coarse grain yields in the 1920s were just over half those in what are now EU countries. The ratio has fallen to about a third, crudely suggesting a shortfall relative to potential, which is also about a third (Koopman 1992). According to the World Bank (1992c), however, the appropriate comparison is with Canada. In the case of wheat, the average yield is lower than Canada's by about 10 percent.

Turning to meat production, Koopman's comparison of average beef and veal production as a proportion of beef cattle inventory size between Eastern Europe and Western Europe suggests that the average in Eastern Europe is lower by about 30 percent. For the former Soviet Union, a comparison of meat yield per animal in the mid-1980s with that achieved in the United States shows a shortfall of 35 percent for beef and 45 percent for pigmeat relative to U.S. averages (Cook 1988 and Koopman 1992, Table 5). Of course, the latter dichotomy is the result of decisions in the former Soviet Union, perhaps rationally motivated by capital scarcity, to increase meat production by raising animal inventories and hence to adopt a more labor-intensive production technology.

In the dairy sector, milk yields per cow are also substantially lower in both Eastern Europe and the former Soviet Union than they are in industrial countries. For Eastern Europe as a whole the average is lower than that for the European Union by about 20 percent, though the discrepancy is larger for the northern countries of the European Union. In the former Soviet Union, milk yields per cow are about half what is achieved in Western Europe and less than half those in the United States (Cook 1988; World Bank 1992c). Finally, the efficiency of livestock feeding is comparatively poor. The Organisation for Economic Cooperation and Development (OECD 1991) is clearest on this, finding that the average former Soviet Union farm spent roughly 75 percent more grain units for milk, 125 percent more for beef, and 70 percent more for mutton. The World Bank (1992b) finds that the overspending on pigmeat was 90 percent and that on poultry meat 70 percent.[20]

This overall picture, summarized in Table 7, suggests that the scope is substantial for food productivity improvements in both Eastern Europe and the former Soviet Union, but especially in the latter. Taken at face value, these results indicate that productivity could increase as much as 50 percent for grains and beef and 25 percent for milk production in Eastern Europe. In the former Soviet Union, grain productivity could increase by 10-50 percent, beef by 50 percent, pigmeat by 80 percent, and milk production by 100 percent. Also in the former Soviet Union, feed use per unit of product could fall by almost 50 percent in both meat and dairy production.

Of course, the potential for improvements in apparent food productivity may be still larger than these numbers imply. This is because the prereform agricultural sector in socialist countries depended on a largely inefficient and backward infrastructure (Johnson 1990; OECD 1991). Two consequences of this were important. First, supplies of inputs were irregular and unpredictable as to volume and quality and hence on-farm productivity was impaired, contributing to the poor comparative

---

[20]These comparisons are based on "oat units", which are the equivalent of 600 grams of starch in the form of grain per unit of meat.

Table 7—Measures of potential food productivity increase in Eastern Europe and the former Soviet Union

Measure	Percent by Which the Productivity Measure in Other Industrial Countries Exceeds That in	
	Eastern Europe	Former Soviet Union
Cereal yields	50	10-50[a]
Meat output per animal slaughtered		
Beef and veal	40	50
Pigmeat	. . .	80
Milk output per cow per year	25	100
Feed efficiency[b]		
Beef and veal	. . .	67
Pigmeat	. . .	80
Milk	. . .	67

Sources: E. Cook, *The Soviet Livestock Sector: Performance and Prospects*, Foreign Agricultural Economic Report No. 235 (Washington, D.C.: U.S. Department of Agriculture, Economic Research Service, 1988); R. B. Koopman, "Agriculture's Role During the Transition from Plan to Market: Real Prices, Real Incentives and Potential Equilibrium," paper prepared for a conference on Economic Statistics for the Economies in Transition: Eastern Europe in the 1990s, U.S. Department of Agriculture, Washington, D.C., 1992; OECD (Organisation for Economic Cooperation and Development), *Agricultural Policies, Markets and Trade: Monitoring and Outlook 1992* (Paris: OECD, 1992); and World Bank, *The Russian Federation: Country Economic Memorandum*, 2 vols. (Washington, D.C.: World Bank, 1992).

[a]Comparison of cereal yields in the former Soviet Union with those in Canada shows a difference of about 10 percent. The larger proportion is based on a restoration of the relativity with Western Europe in the 1920s by Koopman (1992).
[b]Feed efficiency is usually measured as kilograms of meat or liquid milk per kilogram of cereal feed in oat equivalents.

performance just discussed. Second, loss and spoilage rates in storage, transport, and processing are evidently extraordinarily high. According to a recent survey of the food distribution system, the proportion of food lost in the former Soviet Union in the period 1986-90 averaged 14 percent for meat, 28 percent for grain (compared, for example, to 2 percent in the United States), 33 percent for milk, and more than 50 percent for potatoes (Euroconsult 1991).

Given this evidence, the analysis in Chapter 5 depends on assumptions about potential gains in farm-to-retail productivity that are very conservative. Before turning to that analysis, however, it is instructive to review briefly developments in the transition from central planning to market economies being undertaken in Eastern Europe and the former Soviet Union.

4

THE TRANSITION IN THE POSTSOCIALIST ECONOMIES

The literature on the composition and sequencing of reforms in postsocialist economies is now substantial.[21] The elements of transition to a market economy are of three types. The first is macroeconomic stabilization, which requires the unification and deregulation of the exchange rate and the consolidation of the central government's control of the money supply and the government deficit. The second is institutional reform, including the establishment of private property rights, the privatization of government firms, the development of capital and product market infrastructures, and the establishment of social programs to protect those slow to adapt from extreme poverty. And the third is price reform, which includes trade liberalization and domestic market deregulation as well as labor market deregulation.

Although there remains considerable debate as to the sequencing of these reforms, the maintenance of macroeconomic stability is considered essential from the outset (Gelb and Gray 1991). This should be associated with price and trade reforms, including the transition to a convertible current account, to foster foreign investment. Other reforms that are considered desirable early in the transition include small-scale business privatization. This quickly improves the distribution system and hence promotes overall efficiency, but it also provides employment for workers who lose jobs in restructured state-owned corporations. Legal and institutional reform are also early priorities, to protect the property rights of investors in new enterprises. Reforms of the domestic financial sector and the labor market, on the other hand, while important, are evidently inessential at the outset.

Virtually throughout Eastern Europe and the former Soviet Union, new governments have assembled agendas for enactment that are similar to that described. Differences in the sequence followed and the degree of success at each step depend on country-specific political and cultural factors. Although economic performance in the reform period has varied throughout the region, as shown in Table 8, all countries have suffered substantial slumps in output and periods of extremely high inflation.

The political pressure for decentralization has tended to militate against effective fiscal control and the integration of the new markets. This has slowed progress in the former Czechoslovakia, the republics of the former Yugoslavia, and, of course, the former Soviet Union. Moreover, they have suffered under a textbook fallacy of composition. The fact that they have all embarked on reforms simultaneously has changed the external conditions facing each. During the period 1990-91, they dismantled the Council for Mutual Economic Assistance trading system and elected to trade in hard currencies. This disrupted long-term trading arrangements. Postship-

---

[21]See, for example, Blanchard et al. 1991; Gelb and Gray 1991; Murrell 1991a; and Williamson 1991.

Table 8—Change in real gross domestic product (GDP) and the price level in Eastern Europe and the former Soviet Union, 1990-92

Country	Real GDP			Consumer Prices		
	1990	1991	1992	1990	1991	1992
			(percent)			
Eastern Europe	−7	−14	−8	159	119	197
Former Czechoslovakia	...	−16	−9	11	58	11
Hungary	−4	−10	−5	29	37	25
Poland	−12	−7	1	586	70	43
Albania	−10	−28	−8	...	36	226
Bulgaria	−12	−23	−8	26	339	80
Romania	−7	−14	−10	5	161	202
Former Yugoslavia	−8	−17	−24	584	270	15,000
Former Soviet Union	−2	−9	−19	5	95	1,200
Russia	−2	−9	−19	6	93	1,350
Ukraine	−3	−11	−15	4	87	1,090
Estonia	−4	−12	−32	17	211	1,070
Latvia	...	−8	−33	11	124	951
Lithuania	−5	−13	−35	8	225	1,020
Belarus	−3	−1	−11	5	94	1,020
Moldova	−2	−18	−30	6	162	1,270
Armenia	−9	−12	−40	6	100	900
Azerbaijan	−12	−1	−26	8	106	537
Georgia	−12	−21	−46	3	79	913
Kazakhstan	...	−13	−14	4	91	1,380
Kyrgyzstan	4	−5	−25	4	85	855
Tajikistan	−1	−9	−25	6	100	851
Turkmenistan	2	−1	−15	6	113	632
Uzbekistan	4	−1	−10	4	82	700
Total Eastern Europe and former Soviet Union	−3	−17	−15	62	104	829

Source: IMF (International Monetary Fund), *World Economic Outlook,* Washington, D.C.: IMF, 1993), Tables A7 and A13.

ment financing was unavailable, because the risk of nonpayment was too high, and sellers of hard currency goods found better markets for their exports. Trade distortions actually increased as exports were taxed in attempts to restrain inflation, and import-competing industries were subsidized to prevent further declines in home output and employment.

To further complicate matters, the German Democratic Republic disappeared as a trading partner, and trade with Iraq (important to the former Czechoslovakia and Bulgaria) was disrupted. All of these changes adversely affected the terms of trade facing the Eastern European economies (Rodrik 1992; Michalopoulos and Tarr 1992). The terms of trade of the EE-3 with the Balkans and the former Soviet Union declined by 35-50 percent in 1991 alone. At the same time, the volume of EE-3 exports to those regions declined by 75-90 percent. According to Rodrik, these largely external shocks reduced GDP in the former Czechoslovakia and Hungary by at least 7 percent and in Poland by 3.5 percent.

Internally, the Eastern European states are not homogeneous. Some, such as the former Czechoslovakia, are heavily industrialized, with agriculture contributing only 8 percent of GDP, while in others, such as Bulgaria and Romania, agriculture contributes 18 percent. Some, such as Hungary and Poland, had begun to liberalize their economies during the mid-1980s. Others began serious economic reform only after their political liberalization. Accordingly, the former Czechoslovakia and Hungary have succeeded in maintaining an acceptable level of fiscal discipline, while many others have endured periods of extraordinary inflation. Poland, the largest of the group, also seems to have regained macroeconomic stability as of 1991. All three have experienced strong growth in hard currency exports and an associated expansion of the private sector (Collins and Rodrik 1991; IMF 1992b). Despite political tensions associated with the prolonged slump, this pattern should continue, buoyed by Association Agreements with the European Union, which became effective in early 1992 and which ensure that an increasing share of the region's exports enter the European Union at internal EU prices.[22]

In the Balkan states, reforms began later. The continuation of civil war in the largest, the former Yugoslavia, has ensured that there has been no recovery there. Compared with the EE-3, inflation in 1991 was higher in all of the Balkan states and the GDP slump deeper.

Turning to the former Soviet Union, the heterogeneity of its constituent republics is clear from Table 1. Since their reforms began, all of the countries have experienced high inflation and slumps in output. By these measures, the performance of the former Soviet Union in 1991 was, on average, between that of the EE-3 and the Balkans. Their reforms are the more ambitious because they were once part of a single centrally planned economy with a centrally administered infrastructure. Moreover, apart from the tiny Baltic states, market activity and entrepreneurship are more distant in the region's history. The effects on output of the shocks associated with the dismemberment of the Soviet Union and the drive toward market economies have therefore been of a similar order to those in Eastern Europe. While the contraction appears to be bottoming out in the EE-3, that in the Balkan states and the former Soviet Union have further to go, according to the International Monetary Fund (IMF 1992c).

Developments in Agriculture

As output and hence real household income fell in the period immediately following reform in all the postsocialist economies, so did demand for some food products. In the EE-3, old markets for surplus food were lost, and a glut of livestock products developed. This was exacerbated by a shift of consumer demand toward newly available imported foods, which were largely subsidized exports from the European Union. The signing of an "Association Agreement" for agricultural exports to the European Union has offset these trends to some extent, but the expansion of exports under this agreement is being phased in gradually and subject to tight safeguard conditions (Messerlin 1992a; Tangermann 1993). Consequently, the EE-3 countries have reintroduced controls on imported foods, in the form of licensing agreements, quotas, and higher tariffs. The same changes in food consumption and import controls have occurred in the Balkans, although the food glut has been

---

[22]See Messerlin (1992a) and Lundell (1992). These agreements are examined further in Chapter 5.

avoided there. Indeed, there is substantial excess demand for food in Bulgaria and Romania (USDA 1992b, 1992c).

In the former Soviet Union, where food production is especially sensitive to the weather (Desai 1986), the disruptive effects of the dismantling of the Soviet Union on input supplies and product marketing coincided with bad weather in 1991, and crop production fell. Indeed, relative to the prereform trend, grain production was down by one-fourth in Russia and the Ukraine and by more than one-half in Kazakhstan (USDA 1992c; Sheffield 1992). Better weather returned in 1992, but other disruptions are far from fully resolved: the decline in general economic output in the former Soviet Union, combined with increased real income uncertainty at the household level, has led to substitution in consumption of cereal products, including bread, for the more expensive meats and milk products (World Bank 1992c, chap.12).

When most product prices were decontrolled in early 1992, increases in staple food prices were constrained throughout the former Soviet Union. Although the permitted nominal increases measured only in the hundredths of a percent, agriculture's terms of trade have deteriorated. Production of livestock products has fallen, but animal inventories have been slow to decline. Increases in the relative cost of feedgrain have reduced feed efficiency and overall productivity in the sector, while state farms—still unprivatized—seem to be waiting for the historically abundant assistance from governments (World Bank 1992c). Since 1989, the net effect of the transitional changes has been a steady decline in all agricultural imports by the republics of the former Soviet Union, driven largely by reduced final consumption and animal feeding (USDA 1992c, Table 16).

Land reforms have been implemented in most Eastern European countries and have begun in the former Soviet Union In Eastern Europe, these have included programs of landownership restitution, where ownership can be traced to the presocialist period, and changes in farm ownership structure. In the larger economies of Eastern Europe, Poland, and the former Yugoslavia, this has been less important because land had been only partially collectivized under socialism (USDA 1992c). Uncertainties about temporary property rights have retarded planting in Bulgaria, the former Czechoslovakia, Romania, and Hungary, although in the long run these changes should lead to improved land productivity.[23] In the former Soviet Union most food production still occurs on state and collective farms.[24] In the prereform period, private farms occupied only a small percentage of the arable land. Since then, the area under private farms has grown rapidly from its low base, but, in the Russian Federation, transferred land is still less than 10 percent of the cultivated area (USDA 1992c, Table 4). The reestablishment of property rights has been slower in the former Soviet Union because of its longer period under socialism and, consequently, its greater difficulty in establishing historical claims to previously confiscated land. Nonetheless, the new Russian land law, enacted in mid-1993, converts state farms

---

[23]This was certainly the consequence of the "responsibility system" reform in China. See MacMillan, Whalley, and Zhu 1989 and Sicular 1989 and 1991.

[24]The differences between state and collective farms are largely historical. In principle, state farms are state-owned corporations, while collective farms are owned by members. But these differences have few implications for the price incentives faced (World Bank 1992c, Box 12-3).

into collective farms and joint stock companies (Brooks and Lerman 1993). This law also makes possible the subdivision of the former state farms into private plots.

Both in Eastern Europe and the former Soviet Union, the terms of trade facing agriculture are strongly affected by the pricing behavior of firms supplying inputs, on the one hand, and those purchasing products for processing or retail, on the other. As the mainly state-owned corporations that filled these roles are privatized, there is a danger that imperfect competition will impair agriculture's terms of trade because monopoly and monopsony power in these industries will inevitably be greater than at the farm level (Karp and Stefanou 1992). If effective policies on trade practices are not introduced to control this, the boost to food production that would otherwise follow privatization and land reform could be stunted at best. Indeed, recent studies of postreform food market behavior in Russia suggest that markets for food staples are not integrating over distances as small as 200 kilometers (Gardner and Brooks 1994). There is evidence that local officials who retain some control over the movement of food products, with the possible assistance of private elements, have been manipulating food marketing in ways that exacerbate old incentive distortions. Although anticipated reforms to the legal system and the return of centralized control over market behavior should cause this to abate, how long it will take remains a question.

Capital Absorption

Estimates of the drain on world capital markets due to absorption by the postsocialist economies have been as high as US$400 billion per year, but might reasonably be expected to range between US$30 billion and US$100 billion (Collins and Rodrik 1991; Camdessus 1992).[25] To assess the effects on global real interest rates of such increases in capital flows to Eastern Europe and the former Soviet Union, and hence the effects on non-European economies, a disaggregated model of world capital markets is needed. Collins and Rodrik use a parsimonious econometric model for the purpose. They estimate that long-term real interest rates would increase by about 1 percentage point. This, in turn, would reduce net transfers to the developing countries by about US$30 billion per year, the remainder coming from the crowding out of investment in the industrial countries. This cut in resources would lower annual investment in the developing countries by about 0.5 percent of their collective GDP.

Using an advanced global macroeconomic model, McKibbin (1991) addresses the same issue, including an explicit allowance for the capital market effects of the reunification of Germany. For Eastern Europe and the former Soviet Union, he relaxes binding current account constraints (governing financeable deficits) by US$60 billion per year. The combined effect on long-term global real interest rates

---

[25]Collins and Rodrik derive a needs-based estimate of US$420 per year (or 3 percent of the annual output of all industrial countries and 14 percent of their current investment) on the assumption that labor productivity will rise to the current average of industrial countries within 10 years and that the growth in the capital stock needed to achieve this will come from external sources. They discount this estimate, however, on the grounds that the postsocialist countries would not be able to absorb such sums in productive investments, that it would lead to unsustainable increases in external debt, that it ignores technical change (when new technology can be acquired from the West), and, finally, that such investment need not come entirely from external sources.

is an increase of about 3 percentage points, which survives through the decade and fades beyond it. Output would rise in Eastern Europe and the former Soviet Union as well as in Germany, which would increase its imports to Eastern Europe and the former Soviet Union. Output (though not necessarily income) would fall everywhere else. The implications for net transfers to developing countries are less clear from McKibbin's results than from those of the Collins and Rodrik study (1991), but the larger interest rate increase suggests a sharper curtailment of net capital flows.

A decline in net transfers to developing countries of more than US$30 billion per year, should it occur, could well be the most important single consequence for these countries of the economic reforms in Europe and the former Soviet Union. It provides an interesting basis against which to compare the trade effects transmitted through world food markets.

Comparative Advantage and Future Economic Structure

To gauge the ultimate direction of the transition in Eastern Europe and the former Soviet Union, a number of studies have examined the region's physical endowments of primary factors, such as land, labor, human capital, and natural resources; compared them with those of potential trading partners; and attempted to predict the region's pattern of specialization in trade should its economy make a complete transition to markets and private property. For Eastern Europe, such studies suggest exports of agricultural products and manufactures intensive in human capital (CEPR 1990; Collins and Rodrik 1991; Hamilton and Winters 1992b). For the former Soviet Union, Kumi (1992) uses a model in the Heckscher-Ohlin-Vanek tradition. It is implicit in this model that tastes and technology are identical across trading partners and that differences in primary factor endowments are what drives trade. He concludes that, if the former Soviet Union improves its technology to the level of its industrial trading partners, its comparative advantage will be in natural-resource–based goods, including food products.

Anderson (1992; 1993) addresses the same issue, taking the dynamic approach of the "booming sector" literature (Corden 1984). An important point emerging from this literature is that a growing economy's unfolding pattern of trade specialization may not always tend toward the pattern that would apply once it has full technological parity. If technology is more quickly transferred to one tradable goods sector than another, then that sector could boom even if it is not one in which the ultimately developed economy would have a comparative advantage. This is because the sectoral boom draws primary factors from other sectors. Its increased productivity causes a real appreciation, thereby raising costs and reducing relative product prices in other tradable goods sectors and temporarily inhibiting their growth.

In the former Soviet Union, were the minerals and energy sectors to be quickly liberalized and foreign investment in development and further exploration encouraged, the republics better endowed with mineral and energy resources would enjoy investment and export booms. For these reasons, such booms would retard the growth of food production and accelerate the growth in demand for high-value foods, possibly reversing a prior tendency toward net food exports for the former Soviet Union as a whole. But Anderson sees the agricultural sector as having the potential to expand more rapidly than other sectors. This is largely because substantial productivity increases could be realized without extensive foreign direct investment in farming activities. State and cooperative farms function at output levels that are higher than the minimum efficient scale, and their internal organization of labor is very inefficient. Their subdivision into smaller, privately run farms would therefore yield productivity improvements even before the capital stock is revitalized. Paarlberg (1992) reinforces this point in his examination of changes in the East German farm structure.

Nevertheless, the evidence presented by Euroconsult (1991) and OECD (1991) on the food transport, processing, and marketing systems in the former Soviet Union suggests that poor performance in these areas will remain an obstacle to overall food productivity change. Achieving it will require that the trend toward more efficient organizational structures be accompanied by a corresponding trend in the performance of market institutions and infrastructure. Should this occur, apparent consumption will not only fall as wastage is reduced, but large improvements in livestock productivity will be possible at low cost and without the need for extensive foreign direct investment. Such improvements would only require better feed mixtures, a largely recurrent expense, and use of modern breeding technology, which can change the genetic composition of whole herds in one generation.

In the analysis presented in the next chapter, the effects of reforms on other than food production are not directly addressed. Against a reference scenario in which the Eastern European and former Soviet Union economies stagnate, two nonreference scenarios are compared. One assumes a delayed and ultimately slow recovery in food demand and productivity, representing the case in which the agriculture sector lags, and the other assumes a more prompt general recovery, combined with one-off productivity improvements. Apart from this, food demand and supply are assumed to be unaffected by shocks due to reforms in other sectors until the final part of the chapter, where a sensitivity analysis on this assumption is presented. Moreover, the transient macroeconomic shocks associated with the policy transition are not represented explicitly. Clearly, because governments are reluctant to allow food prices to rise with the general price level, the recovery in agriculture is vulnerable to macroeconomic instability in this period (Brooks 1993). The analysis focuses, instead, on the economic environment of food production in the region before the reform and its likely counterpart after the transition. The understanding is implicit throughout that the disruption due to nationalist conflicts will abate and that no return to isolated totalitarian political regimes with centrally planned economies is considered.

5

ANALYSIS OF FOOD POLICY REFORMS

The range of possible implications of reforms in European and former Soviet Union countries for international trade in food is most conveniently assessed by quantitative analysis. Even though there is considerable uncertainty about the behavior of households and firms in the former centrally planned economies and about new political shocks in those economies, a coherent quantitative analysis based on available information can help to assess the comparative likelihood of alternative international trade scenarios, and to define the scope of possible outcomes. To this end, an established model of international trade in food commodities has been updated and adapted. The unfolding of events in the wider economies of East and Central Europe and the former Soviet Union is depicted in three extreme scenarios. Policy reforms in the agricultural sectors of these economies and their international implications are then examined in the context of each scenario.

Europe and the Former Soviet Union
in a Global Food Trade Model

To examine the effects of economic reform in any one region on the behavior of world food markets, a model of world food market behavior is needed. A number of such models now exist, each with its own advantages.[26] The model used in this report is that developed by Tyers and Anderson (1992). Its special advantage is that it characterizes the two main components of most food policy regimes: the pure protection component, which boosts incentives to produce food by raising expected relative product prices, and the pure insulation component, which reduces price risk in domestic food markets by insulating them from international price volatility. The latter is useful because agricultural product markets are comparatively risky, and risk preferences motivate much food policy intervention (Tyers 1991). Its use, however, requires a fully dynamic model that incorporates the behavior of risk-sensitive agents such as stockholders. Accordingly, the model includes endogenous stockholding, and it differentiates between the short- and the long-run responses inherent in farm production and government intervention in food markets.

Although fully dynamic models such as this are particularly appropriate for examining the path of adjustment taken following unforeseen shocks to production or food policy, it is also of interest for estimating the net effects on prices and

---

[26]See, for example, Zietz and Valdés 1988; Roningen 1986; Parikh et al. 1988; OECD 1990; and Burniaux and van der Mensbrugge 1990.

quantities following full adjustment by farmers and policymakers. For this purpose, there is also a static version of the model, which calculates unique full-adjustment partial equilibria for each year on a simulated path. The sequence of such equilibria can be used to represent the path food markets might take had some hypothetical policy regime always been in place, or simply to abstract from short-run fluctuations and focus on the underlying full-adjustment response to some phased policy reform. The model therefore works in both the dynamic and static modes.

To keep the model manageable, attention is restricted to the major traded food staples, namely wheat, coarse grain, rice, ruminant meat (mainly cattle and sheep), nonruminant meat (pigs and poultry), dairy products, and sugar. These seven commodity groups account for about half of world trade in food, with edible oils and other oilseed products and beverages accounting for most of the rest (Tyers and Anderson 1992, 17). The model is highly disaggregated across countries, however. In the newly updated version there are 35 countries and country groups, of which Europe and the former Soviet Union make up 10, and 18 are developing economies. These countries and country groups are listed in Table 9.

Unlike the models by Parikh et al.(1988) and Burniaux and van der Mensbrugge (1990), the Tyers-Anderson model is not economy-wide. It excludes the markets for other traded goods, services, and the factors of production. National income, interest rates, and real currency exchange rates therefore enter as exogenous variables. Given that this study is concerned with the agricultural consequences of reforms, and that great uncertainty surrounds both the reforms and the responses to them in the wider economies of Eastern Europe and the former Soviet Union, research economy suggests that nonagricultural developments be represented by multiple exogenous scenarios.[27]

As in the other global models, marketing and infrastructural margins are represented only crudely in this model. A reversal in the direction of trade, for example, does not alter the relationship between domestic and border prices. Where infrastructure is particularly poor, as in some of the republics of the former Soviet Union, this abstraction can lead the model to overestimate the volume of trade following a reversal in its direction. The error associated with this abstraction is not serious in practice, however, for two reasons. First, while it is of obvious importance in the hypothetical case of a perfectly homogeneous commodity (the assumption of homogeneity in this model notwithstanding), the food commodities considered here are not truly homogeneous and, even where net imports or exports are large, there is usually some trade in both directions. Reversals of net trade direction then indicate a scaling up of the trade in one direction relative to the other. Since the volumes consumed and produced are generally much larger than those traded, average home prices need not change much due to such shifts in the composition of consumption or production. Second, where a change of net trade direction occurs in a whole region, such as the former Soviet Union, it need not imply any change in net trade direction for the constituent republics.

---

[27]Although information economy is achieved by focusing on the food sector and characterizing events in the wider economy in the form of scenarios, one important disadvantage of this approach is that the effects of policy reform on incomes in the agricultural sector do not feed back into shifts in the demand curves for food. This is not a problem where the agricultural sector is a small part of the overall economy. But, where it is large, as in Central Asia, the net trade results need to be interpreted with caution.

Table 9—Countries, country groups, and commodities identified in the model

Regions
Industrial market economies
   1. Australia
   2. New Zealand
   3. Canada
   4. United States
   5. EU-12[a]
   6. EFTA-5[b]
   7. Japan
Eastern Europe
   8. Northeast Europe or EE-3 (former
      Czechoslovakia, Hungary, Poland)
   9. Balkans (Albania, Bulgaria, Romania,
      Yugoslavia)
Former Soviet Union
   10. Russia
   11. Ukraine
   12. Baltic States (Estonia, Latvia, Lithuania)
   13. Western republics (Armenia,
       Azerbaijan, Belarus, Georgia, Moldova)
   14. Kazakhstan
   15. Central Asia (Kyrgyzstan, Tajikistan,
       Turkmenistan, Uzbekistan)
Asian developing countries
   16. Korea, Republic of
   17. Taiwan
   18. China, mainland
   19. Indonesia
   20. Philippines

Asian developing countries (continued)
   21. Thailand
   22. Bangladesh
   23. India
   24. Pakistan
   25. Other Asian countries
Latin America
   26. Argentina
   27. Brazil
   28. Mexico
   29. Cuba
   30. Other Latin American
       countries
Africa
   31. Egypt
   32. Nigeria
   33. South Africa
   34. Other Sub-Saharan African countries
   35. Other North African and Middle
       Eastern countries
Commodities
   1. Rice
   2. Wheat
   3. Coarse grain
   4. Sugar
   5. Dairy products
   6. Ruminant meat
   7. Nonruminant meat

[a]EU-12 are the countries now belonging to the European Union: Belgium, Denmark, France, Germany, Greece, Ireland, Italy, Luxembourg, the Netherlands, Portugal, Spain, and the United Kingdom.
[b]EFTA-5 includes the continental members of the European Free Trade Association: Austria, Finland, Norway, Sweden, and Switzerland.

If the change is from net deficit to net surplus, a common underlying pattern has net surpluses rising in some republics and net deficits falling in others.

A complete mathematical description of the updated model is provided in Appendix 1. Included in the model, but not discussed in the appendix, is a set of welfare measures. These are equivalent variations in income that approximate the income equivalents of policy-induced departures from reference prices for farmers and consumers. The measures are fully documented in Tyers and Anderson 1992, Appendix 1.

The parameters of the model were originally estimated from time series data for the period 1962-82. Most of the key econometric results for this interval are discussed in Tyers 1984. Since these estimates were made, the parameter set has been revised to accommodate results from more detailed and up-to-date studies as they emerge in the literature. Most recently, the quantity database has been updated to 1990, as have the estimates of the pure protection components of agricultural policies.[28] Simulations begin in 1991, stepping off from a base period in which nontrending variables (such as prices) are set at an average over 1986-90 and trending variables (such as income and production) are set at trend levels in 1990.[29] The key behavioral parameters for consumption, production, and storage remain the same for most countries (see Tyers and Anderson 1992, Appendix 2). Although the formulation of the model does not use trade elasticities explicitly, estimates are implicit in the model's trade volume responses to changes in the international terms of trade. These implicit values are presented in Tyers and Anderson 1989.

For the new country groups of Eastern Europe and the former Soviet Union, data are clearly insufficient to estimate complete sets of behavioral parameters. In some cases, judgmental values chosen by specialists in this region have been adopted. In others, key parameter values have been borrowed from the databases for what are considered similar agricultural economies in Western Europe and Asia.[30] The complete set of parameters for Europe and the former Soviet Union are tabulated in a supplement to this report available on request from the International Food Policy Research Institute.

Growth Scenarios for the Postsocialist Economies

Because the path of political reforms and the response to changes in economic policy in the postsocialist economies is not readily predictable, the best approach is to examine a variety of disparate scenarios. These are constructed with a view to encapsulating the ultimate course of these economies while delimiting the range of possible outcomes by ensuring that the assumptions behind each are feasible. Each embodies assumptions about the growth path of real household income, food produc-

---

[28]The updates of the quantity database draw on data for grain production, trade, and stocks provided by the Economic Research Service of USDA and from the food balance sheet tapes from the Food and Agriculture Organization of the United Nations (FAO). These data were acquired and processed by the International Economic Data Bank of the Australian National University. The revised prereform price distortions are discussed in detail in Chapter 3. They are from estimates of producer and consumer subsidy equivalents by the OECD (statistics are available on microcomputer diskette to supplement OECD 1992), by USDA (Webb, Lopez, and Penn 1990 and more recent estimates, particularly for Eastern Europe and the former Soviet Union provided to the author by the Europe Branch of the Agricultural Trade Analysis Division of USDA, as summarized in Koopman 1992).

[29]Base-period levels of real household income and food production, consumption, and trade in each country are set for 1990 as fitted values from geometric time trends over the 1980s. The process is partly judgmental, the objective being to remove any extraordinary departures from trends in the data for 1990. In many of the postsocialist countries, substantial declines in real household income and food quantities had already occurred by 1990. In these cases, benchmark values are used, the reform-induced declines being introduced as exogenous shocks in the first year each time postsocialist reform is simulated. The income estimates, for example, therefore differ from the 1990 values drawn from current sources and presented in Table 1 of Chapter 3.

[30]Key elasticities of demand and supply for Eastern Europe and the former Soviet Union were drawn from compendia such as Sullivan et al. (1992) and the work of the regional specialists at the USDA Economic Research Service, supplied personally. Where authoritative estimates of such parameters were unavailable, values were adopted from the databases for like agricultural economies elsewhere in Europe and Asia. These values were then modified for consistency with the patterns of production and expenditure in Eastern Europe and the former Soviet Union.

tivity, and the efficiency with which feedgrains are used in livestock production. The complete set of assumed growth rates of real household income and food productivity is documented in Appendix 2, Table 21. What follows is an illustrative summary.

Of the three scenarios defined, the first simply provides a reference against which policy reforms and the other scenarios can be compared. It assumes complete economic stagnation in the postsocialist economies from the base period (1986-90) onward. There is no growth in per capita real income, no change in food productivity, and no improvement in feeding efficiency. The second, the low-growth scenario, incorporates the declines in real disposable household income and food output from the base period through the early part of 1993 (drawing mainly on IMF 1993 for real income shocks and Sheffield 1992 and USDA 1992b and 1992c for production shocks). Thereafter, the EE-3 and the Baltic states are assumed to recover somewhat and then to settle into economic growth at rates similar to those achieved in the prereform period. The Balkans and the rest of the former Soviet Union stagnate for another year and then resume modest growth. The pattern of food productivity change in the three regions follows that of income. After the shocks of the early 1990s, normal indigenous technical improvements continue, increasing output at the prereform or benchmark rate, as happens in all other economies represented in the model. No improvements in feeding efficiency take place.

The third, the high-growth scenario, is more optimistic after 1992, both as to the pace of the economy-wide recovery and the performance of the food sector. Real household disposable income growth is arbitrarily (but optimistically) set at rates sufficient to permit the economies to catch up with the extrapolated benchmark trend (Figures 1 and 2). The corresponding set of assumptions about food productivity

Figure 1— Exogenous income projections, Eastern Europe, 1990-2010

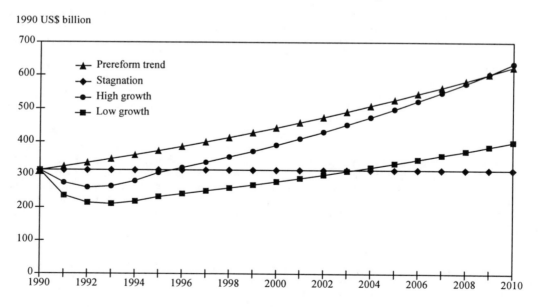

1990 US$ billion

Source: Based on the data and assumptions delineated in Appendix 2, Table 21.

Figure 2— Exogenous income projections, former Soviet Union, 1990-2010

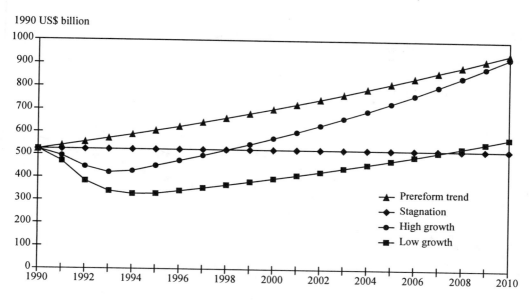

1990 US$ billion

Source: Based on the data and assumptions delineated in Appendix 2, Table 21.

again depends on benchmark growth rates, as indicated in Appendix 2, Table 21. Rather than have productivity growth resume at the benchmark rates, as in the low-growth scenario, the rates in the high-growth scenario are actually chosen to outpace the benchmark trend. The added boost to productivity represents the adoption of superior farm management practices and technology from the West, particularly in the livestock sectors. The implications for the path of total food output in the EE-3 and Russia are shown in Figures 3 and 4.

The substantial differences in productivity between the agricultures of Western Europe and the postsocialist economies were documented in Chapter 3. The boost assumed in the high-growth scenario (Table 10) is modest compared with the implied potential (Table 7). The anticipated gains in Eastern Europe and the former Soviet Union are the same for all foods except dairy products, where the potential for improvement from better management and technology seems comparatively large in the former Soviet Union. As is appropriate in a high-growth scenario, the assumption is implicit that the former Soviet Union is able to meet at least some of Cook's (1988) preconditions for the realization of its livestock potential: namely that farms become more autonomous, choosing production levels unilaterally and retaining any profits (or losses); that primary factor prices become more market-driven; and that efficient livestock farms be permitted to specialize. The corresponding increases in feeding efficiency are also listed in Table 11. Feed efficiency in Eastern Europe is projected to improve to the level of that in Western Europe, while most of the former Soviet Union is projected to traverse about half that gap. The comparatively isolated regions of Kazakhstan and Central Asia achieve more modest improvements.

Figure 3— Exogenous component of staple food production, EE-3, 1990-2010

1990 US$ billion

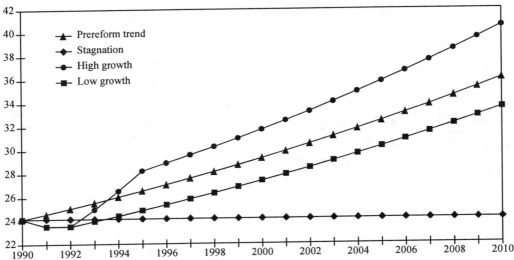

Source: Based on the data and assumptions delineated in Appendix 2, Table 21.
Notes: Production of grains, livestock products, and sugar is valued at 1990 world prices. The EE-3 countries are the former Czechoslovakia, Hungary, and Poland.

Figure 4— Exogenous component of staple food production, Russia, 1990-2010

1990 US$ billion

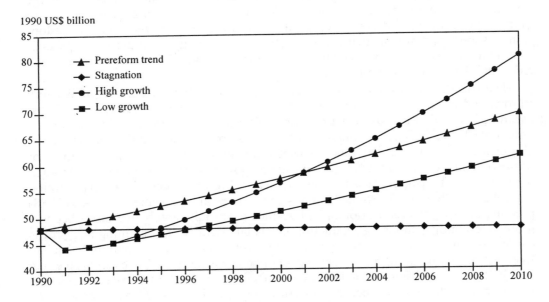

Source: Based on the data and assumptions delineated in Appendix 2, Table 21.
Note: Production of grains, livestock products, and sugar is valued at 1990 world prices.

34

Table 10— Relative productivity gains in final production in the high-growth scenario compared with the prereform trend

Commodity	Eastern Europe	Former Soviet Union
	(percent)	
Rice	10	10
Wheat	10	10
Coarse grain	5	5
Sugar	5	5
Dairy products	20	50
Ruminant meat	20	20
Nonruminant meat	20	20

Source: Conservative estimates of potential, based on the data provided in Table 7.
Note: This table shows the proportions by which supply curves are shifted to the right (output rises for given input use).

The Reference Simulation

To provide a basis for comparison, one simulation of the seven global food markets extends from 1990 through 2010 on the assumption that policy regimes are stable throughout the world and that, while underlying income and productivity growth continues in most economies, those of Eastern Europe and the former Soviet Union remain stagnant throughout. Food production and consumption in the former Soviet Union change during this period only in response to any changes in the domestic terms of trade that are transmitted from abroad by their price policy

Table 11— Feedgrain use per unit of output (by weight) in the high-growth versus the low-growth scenario

Region/Scenario	Dairy Products	Ruminant Meat	Nonruminant Meat
Eastern Europe			
Low growth	0.6	9.0	5.5
High growth[a]	0.4	6.0	4.5
Former Soviet Union[b]			
Low growth	0.8	12.0	7.0
High growth[c]	0.6	9.0	5.0
Kazakhstan and Central Asia			
Low growth	0.8	12.0	7.0
High growth[c]	0.7	10.0	6.0

Source: Feed use statistics are drawn from the sources cited in Table 7. Improvements embodied in the high-growth scenario are conservative estimates of the potential suggested in Table 7.
Note: Feed efficiency is usually measured as kilograms of meat or liquid milk per kilogram of cereal feed in oat equivalents.
[a]For the EE-3 the efficiency improvements in the high-growth scenario, relative to the low-growth scenario, are phased in over 1993-96.
[b]Excludes Kazakhstan and Central Asia
[c]High-growth efficiency gains in Kazakhstan and Central Asia are phased in over 1994-2010.

regimes. The simulation does not include unilateral policy reforms to which some Western industrial countries are now committed, nor any reforms that might emerge from the Uruguay Round of international trade negotiations. The resulting paths of international food prices are illustrated in Figure 5.

For the most part, prices remain fairly stable. Only dairy product prices have any significant trend, and this reflects the gradual implementation of new technology, mainly in the large dairy sectors of Western Europe and North America, which remain both highly protected and highly insulated. The trend of the past two decades toward food surpluses in industrial countries and deficits in the developing and postsocialist countries continues. The self-sufficiency ratio for industrial countries as a group rises from 1.07 in the base period to 1.20 by 2000. Those for developing and postsocialist countries fall from 0.97 to 0.90 and from 0.95 to 0.94, respectively.[31]

Against this reference simulation, the analysis first compares unilateral reforms in the European Union and the proposed expansion of the European Union to include the EFTA countries. Once this is completed, however, the new simulation, incorporating partial reforms and EU expansion, is used as a point of comparison for the effects of economic changes in the postsocialist economies.

Figure 5— Reference international food prices, 1990-2010

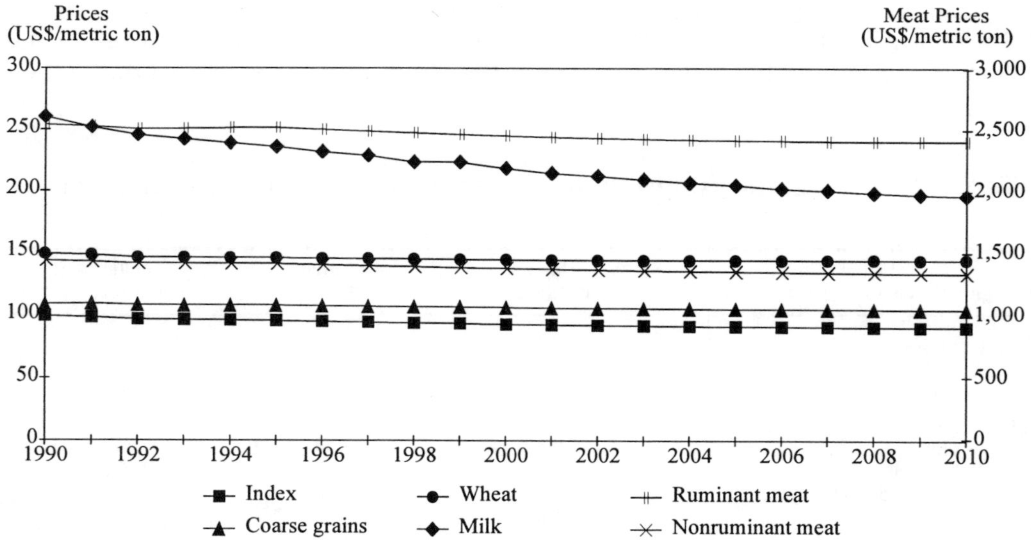

Source: Results from the analysis using the model described in Appendix 1.

---

[31]The self-sufficiency ratio referred to here is the value of domestic output at base period world prices divided by the value of domestic consumption at the same world prices.

Unilateral EU Reform and EU Expansion

In May 1992 the European Union adopted, with slight modification, the reform package associated with the name of former EC Commissioner for Agriculture Ray MacSharry (Commission of the European Communities 1991). Over three years, beginning in 1993, the package will reduce the farm prices of cereals, oilseeds, and other protein crops by approximately 35 percent. Cereal farmers will be compensated with partially decoupled payments, but commercial farmers (producers of at least 92 tons of equivalent output) will need to set aside 15 percent of their land. In the livestock sector, the major reform is a reduction of the beef price by 15 percent, compensated in part by subsidies per head for the culling of the herd. At the time this report was written no reform of the sugar policy, beyond the existing two-tier pricing system, was proposed nor had any substantial reform of the dairy policy been agreed to.

In this analysis of unilateral CAP reform a number of simplifications are made. First, reductions in EU consumer cereal prices are assumed to be 35 percent, irrespective of any resulting change in international trading prices. Second, the compensation of commercial cereal farmers is in the form of payments that are fixed in terms of area planted and base-period regional average yields. Depending on how this is implemented, it might be profitable for farmers to reduce variable inputs and hence output. In this analysis, grain supply elasticities are left unchanged, while supply curves are shifted so as to reduce output by 10 percent (the net effect of a possible 15 percent land set-aside less 5 percent slippage).[32] Beef producer and consumer prices are reduced by 15 percent, again irrespective of any response in the international market. No changes are introduced to either dairy or sugar policy, except that dairy production is assumed to remain constrained by quotas.[33]

The impact of this reform is assessed by making a new simulation that incorporates the reforms for each of the 20 years through 2010. The static version of the model is used to provide an estimate of the deviation of the full-adjustment path, following the reform from the original reference simulation. The results are summarized for the year 2000 in Table 12. The policy changes reduce EU production of cereals and meat and increase their domestic consumption. The European Union's excess supply of these commodities declines and world prices rise. The opposite is true for the international prices of nonruminant meats, since farmers in the European Union switch their resources out of beef and into these products, and consumers switch their demand from nonruminants to beef and cereal products, collectively increasing the European Union's excess supply.

As expected, in that year, the production of cereals and ruminant meats is lower with the reform than it would be without it, and the European Union's net trade in these

---

[32]Haley, Herlihy, and Johnson (1991) discuss "slippage" in the context of their approach to estimating the production effects of land set-aside programs in the United States. The rate of one-third assumed here is probably high, but so is the set-aside rate of 15 percent, since this is strictly to apply only to "large" farmers. The assumption of a net 10 percent shift in supply seems as robust as might be expected a priori.

[33]The EU dairy quota constraint is imposed by fixing production and solving for the corresponding supply price. The difference between that supply price and the CAP price is then transferred to producers as rent. Earlier studies by CARD (1992a), Josling and Tangermann (1992), and the Centre for World Food Studies (Folmer et al. 1993) offer slightly more faithful representations of the unilateral reforms as they were originally proposed.

Table 12— Effects of unilateral reform in the European Union on production and net trade in 2000

Policy Change	Rice	Wheat	Coarse Grain	Sugar	Dairy Products[a]	Ruminant Meat	Non-ruminant Meat
			(percent)				
Change in international price, 2000							
Reform over reference	4.0	7.0	5.0	0.7	0.3	5.0	−1.0
Production growth, 2000 over 1990							
Reference	16.0	30.0	19.0	23.0	19.0	20.0	30.0
Reform	5.0	16.0	10.0	22.0	19.0	5.0	44.0
Change in production							
Reform over reference	−9.0	−11.0	−8.0	−0.4	0.0	−12.0	11.0
			(million metric tons)				
Change in net exports[b]							
Reform over reference	−0.5	−17.9	−9.0	−0.0	−0.0	−2.2	3.6

Source: Results from the analysis using the model described in Appendix 1.

[a]EU-12 dairy production is assumed to be quota constrained to avoid increases due to the (partially transmitted) rise in the international price.

[b]In 2000 the European Union is actually projected to be a net importer of rice and coarse grain. Where positive, a change in "net exports" indicates increased exports or a reduction in net imports, depending on which prevailed in the reference case.

products shifts in the direction of net imports. Notably, however, even with the reform, production of these products in 2000 is substantially higher than in the base period. The reform serves only to retard the *growth* in EU production, not to reduce its level. Output of nonruminant meats grows more rapidly as resources move into these unreformed sectors, and so, for all of the GLS products, the European Union's self-sufficiency remains high at 111 percent. This is higher than its base-period level (105 percent), though it is smaller than its reference level for the year 2000 (116 percent).

The other substantial reform in Western Europe that will directly affect international food markets is the admission of the EFTA countries to the European Union. Agriculture in these countries has been highly protected, even compared with the European Union (Table 4), so that EU membership should eventually reduce their food production and increase their food consumption. This trend is likely to be more pronounced because of the ongoing unilateral reforms in the European Union. Concordance of EFTA agricultural policy regimes with the reformed CAP is likely to be phased in over several years. Here, this is assumed to take effect between 1992 and 1996, coinciding roughly with those unilateral reforms. It is readily introduced in a third (static) model simulation, one combining the EU unilateral reforms with EFTA membership. In this simulation, EFTA price distortions follow a linear path between their levels in 1992 and those of the Union in 1996. Dairy producers in the EU-12 are still constrained by quotas, even after the EFTA dairy industry reduces its output as its protection levels decline to the EU-12 level. The effects of this constraint, combined with unilateral EU reform, are summarized in Figure 6. The levels of all GLS international prices are 3-4 percent higher than before.

Figure 6— World price changes as a result of unilateral reforms and EFTA membership in the European Union, 1990-2010

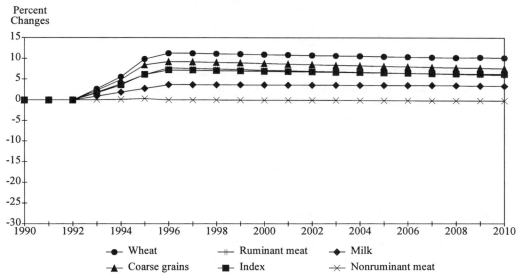

Source: Results from the analysis using the model described in Appendix 1.
Note: EFTA is the European Free Trade Association.

Closer Economic Ties between the EE-3 and the European Union

Although the possibility that the former Czechoslovakia, Hungary, and Poland might join the European Union has been discussed (Hamilton and Winters 1992a; Messerlin 1992b), the comparative size and present poverty of their collective economy are factors that weigh against this happening soon. Nevertheless, steps have been taken toward bringing the agricultural sectors of these countries under the CAP. These take the form of Association Agreements, which became effective in early 1992 (Lundell 1992; Messerlin 1992a; and Tangermann 1993). Barriers to all trade in the EE-3 were almost eliminated unilaterally as part of their early reforms (Messerlin 1992a). More recently, however, farm subsidies and export restitutions have been implemented in unilateral moves by the EE-3 to bring their agricultural policies into greater harmony with those in the European Union (Swinnen 1992). Since these agreements commit the European Union to gradual reductions in the distortions imposed against these countries' exports, including their agricultural exports, they will increasingly reduce the domestic cost of EE-3 agricultural support.

Although the agreements restrain the growth in agricultural exports through phased quantitative restrictions and safeguard clauses, the reductions in tariffs and levies are as high as 60 percent over three years. They represent a "foot in the door" for EE-3 farmers, who will receive intra-EU prices for an increasing share of their products.

Improvements in agricultural production incentives in the EE-3, associated with this access to EU markets, combined with the potential for productivity increases, could boost food supplies in Europe substantially. To assess this, the next simulation adds to the unilateral reforms in the European Union and EFTA membership the full conformity of the agricultural policy of the EE-3 with the reformed CAP, phased in over the interval 1990–2010. In this simulation it is assumed that the policy transition in the EE-3 is from prereform domestic prices to EU prices and that this transition takes place linearly over the two decades. Of course, this is very much an abstraction of actual events in the EE-3, which include a shock liberalization across all sectors, followed by a gradual expansion of trade with the European Union.

The most significant aspect of the policy transition thus assumed concerns the dairy sector. Although the EE-3 average hides some heterogeneity of prereform dairy policy (Table 4), on the whole, dairy farms were not protected in the prereform sector and dairy consumption was subsidized. The change to EU prices therefore brings about a massive shift in incentives facing EE-3 dairy producers and consumers. Without quota constraints, the region's excess supply of dairy products can be expected to increase substantially, depressing international prices. Tyers (1993) examines the magnitude of this unconstrained excess supply. Because it is large, however, concordance of agricultural policy in the EE-3 with that in the European Union is sure to bring with it quota constraints on dairy production, whether or not the region actually joins the European Union. In the analysis that follows a dairy quota is applied that restricts increases in EE-3 production to no more than 25 percent over the 1990 level.

Next, a new simulation is carried out in which reforms in Western Europe are combined with the changes in the EE-3 as well as with the income and productivity shocks associated with general economic change there (Figures 1 and 3). This simulation is compared with one that incorporates only the effects of unilateral reforms in Western Europe. The incremental effects of economic change and CAP conformity in the EE-3 alone are summarized in Table 13. Higher domestic producer and consumer food prices, combined with reduced purchasing power, cause reductions in direct food consumption and substantial increases in production and the derived demand for feedgrains. Net exports of livestock products increase. In the low-growth scenario, feedgrain demand increases sufficiently to move EE-3 grain trade toward net imports. In the high-growth scenario improved feeding efficiency and overall food productivity move the region toward net surplus in all GLS markets. Net dairy product exports increase most, in spite of a production quota limiting the rise in output to no more than 25 percent.

The fiscal consequences of the extension of the CAP beyond the EU-12 to farmers in both EFTA and the EE-3 can be approximated from the simulations thus far. The approximation is a crude one, since all distortions are converted in the model to equivalent ad valorem tariffs or export subsidies, which then determine their consequences for government revenue and expenditure. The results, given in Table 14, suggest that the reductions in protection that would accompany EFTA membership would bring substantial savings. By the year 2000, however, the greater part of these savings would be lost with entry of the EE-3 into the European Union.[34]

---

[34]Government expenditures associated with higher prices in the quota-constrained dairy sector include a lump sum transfer, as suggested in footnote 33. The welfare consequences of EU expansion are considered by Anderson and Tyers (1993) in greater detail, using the same model.

Table 13—Incremental effects of economic change in the EE-3, combined with conformity with the reformed Common Agricultural Policy (CAP) of the European Union, 2000

Economic Change	Rice	Wheat	Coarse Grain	Sugar	Dairy Products[a]	Ruminant Meat	Non-ruminant Meat
			(percent)				
Effect on world prices							
Low growth[b]	−0.2	−0.5	0.1	−1.2	−6.5	−1.2	−1.4
High growth[b]	−1.9	−3.4	−3.5	−1.9	−5.8	−3.1	−2.9
Change in 2000 production							
Low growth	26.0	21.0	27.0	19.0	26.0	13.0	44.0
High growth	38.0	34.0	50.0	28.0	25.0	46.0	78.0
Change in consumption							
Low growth	−11.0	16.0	49.0	−1.0	−13.0	−7.0	2.0
High growth	−4.0	14.0	43.0	4.0	−7.0	0.4	7.0
Change in net exports[c]			(million metric tons)				
Low growth	0.0	1.3	−7.1	0.6	10.0	0.2	2.0
High growth	0.0	4.7	1.2	0.7	8.1	0.6	3.4

Source: Results from the analysis using the model described in Appendix 1.

Notes: EE-3 includes the former Czechoslovakia, Hungary, and Poland. These results examine the incremental effect of EE-3 farmers coming under the CAP. The reference simulation in this case includes unilateral reform and expansion of the European Union to include the European Free Trade Association countries. This simulation is compared with one in which these reforms are included, along with the extension of the CAP to all EE-3 farmers and the income and productivity shocks associated with the wider economic reform of the EE-3 economy.

[a]Dairy production in the EE-3 is assumed to be constrained by quotas so that output cannot increase by more than 25 percent over its 1990 level.

[b]The low- and high-growth scenarios here refer only to the EE-3. In these simulations, the economies of the Balkans and the former U.S.S.R. remain stagnant.

[c]In 2000 the EE-3 is actually projected to be a net importer of cereals and sugar and a net exporter of livestock products. Where positive, a change in "net exports" indicates increased exports or a reduction in net imports, depending on which prevailed in the reference case.

Table 14—Effects on government expenditure of enlargement of the European Union, 2000 (expenditure savings relative to the reference scenario)

Scenario	EU-12	EFTA	EE-3	Total
		(1990 US$ billion)		
CAP reform only in EC-12	4	−1	0	3
CAP reform and EFTA membership	4	32	0	36
CAP reform and membership of EFTA and EE-3, low growth	5	32	−28	9
CAP reform and membership of EFTA and EE-3, high growth	6	32	−34	4

Source: Results from the analysis using the model described in Appendix 1.

Notes: CAP is the Common Agricultural Policy of the European Union. The EU-12 countries comprise Belgium, Denmark, France, Germany, Greece, Ireland, Italy, Luxembourg, the Netherlands, Portugal, Spain, and the United Kingdom. EFTA is the European Free Trade Association countries (Austria, Finland, Iceland, Norway, Sweden, and Switzerland). EE-3 is the former Czechoslovakia, Hungary, and Poland.

Membership here connotes conformity of agricultural policies with the CAP. Dairy production is assumed to be constrained by quotas in the European Union when EFTA's entry raises external prices. Entry by the EE-3 greatly raises internal milk prices there. Production is constrained not to expand by more than 25 percent.

Moreover, full conformity is assumed to take two decades, at the end of which substantial further CAP reforms will be needed to prevent a net expansion of its budget impact.

The international price effects of EE-3 reform with high growth are charted over the two-decade, phase-in period (Figure 7). Two important points emerge. First, the production-enhancing effects of the reform are dominant only in the first decade. Thereafter the strength of the economic recovery in the region is sufficient to ensure that demand growth largely offsets further improvements in food productivity. Second, the international price effects are opposite in direction to the effects of the reforms in Western Europe (Figure 6) and more than half their magnitude. The net effects on world food markets of pan-European reform are therefore likely to be small. Any substantial change in world food markets will therefore depend on changes in the food markets of the Balkans and the former Soviet Union.

Economic Policy Reform in the Balkans and the Former Soviet Union

The sweeping political reforms began earlier in the EE-3, and they have not been as turbulent and economically disruptive as in the Balkans and the former Soviet Union (see Chapter 4). The paths their economic recovery are likely to take are therefore even more uncertain than those for the EE-3. Nevertheless, as discussed in Chapter 4, it is the stated intent of most governments in the former Soviet Union to

Figure 7— Incremental world price changes, as a result of EE-3 reforms, 1990-2010

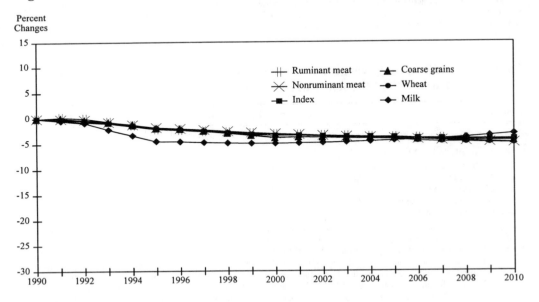

Source: Results from the analysis using the model described in Appendix 1.
Note: The EE-3 countries are the former Czechoslovakia, Hungary, and Poland.

move toward market-driven economies with fewer incentive distortions. Therefore, the case in which all prereform incentive distortions are phased out throughout the region is simulated. A complete liberalization of this type is unlikely in so heterogeneous a region, but the prospects of a leveling of the playing field facing food production are enhanced by the perception, stemming from the Chinese experience, that quick gains in agricultural GDP might be possible as a result.[35] Such a liberalization, then, forms the basis of the experiment to be conducted here. Two simulations are carried out, both incorporating the transition economic shocks (Figures 2 and 4) and a five-year phased liberalization of all incentive distortions facing food production and consumption (1991-95). They differ only in that one has the low-growth recovery in which there are no extraordinary productivity gains and the other the high-growth recovery, embodying the gains detailed in Table 10.

The prereform incentive distortions in the former Soviet Union assisted both producers and consumers, on average (Table 4). In general, then, a liberalization would be expected to lead to lower consumption and production with the effects on net trade depending on the sizes of the distortions and the elasticities of response of producers and consumers. It is instructive, however, to note that the livestock sectors were highly assisted relative to grains, so that the balancing effect of a liberalization is to raise grain production and reduce livestock production and therefore feedgrain demand. On the consumption side, prereform distortions appear to have subsidized grain consumption more effectively than meats and dairy products. The corresponding effect of a liberalization on consumption is therefore to reduce direct grain demand relative to demand for livestock products. Because the demand for grain as feed and for direct consumption can be expected to fall, while its relative producer price is likely to rise, it is clear that a move toward a net surplus in grain is an inevitable outcome irrespective of assumptions about the strength of any postreform recovery.

The results from the two simulations are summarized in Table 15, which lists the estimated incremental effects of food liberalization in the Balkans and the former Soviet Union by the year 2000, detailing changes in food consumption, production, and trade in Russia. The corresponding changes in the other states of the region are detailed in Appendix 2, Table 22.

As expected, food consumption tends to fall. Direct consumption of dairy products and cattle and sheep meat falls the most. Consumers substitute poultry and pigmeat, the prices of which rise by substantially less in the course of the liberalization. Indirect grain consumption also falls in the low-growth case because livestock production falls when assistance is removed, product prices fall, while grain input prices rise. In the high-growth case, however, livestock production rises in spite of the adverse shift in the terms of trade because of productivity improvements embodied in that scenario. Indirect grain demand still falls, again because of improvements in feeding efficiency (Table 11). Overall, the dominant effect on the region's net trade is a shift to a

---

[35]On the other hand, the emergence of a well-organized agricultural lobby, akin to that in Western Europe, is a possibility. Prior to the 1993 Russian elections, for example, the qualifying party with the largest collection of signatures was the Agrarian Party (*Economist* 1993b), though this might simply reflect the still substantial influence of the management of state farms. The possibility that the food policies of the Balkans and the former Soviet Union might ultimately conform with those of Western Europe is considered in Tyers 1993.

Table 15— Incremental effects on Russian food production, consumption, and trade of economic change combined with food price reforms in the Balkans and the former Soviet Union, 2000

Effect	Rice	Wheat	Coarse Grain	Sugar	Dairy Products[a]	Ruminant Meat	Non-ruminant Meat
				(percent)			
Effect on world prices							
Low growth[a]	−11	−20	−16	−1	−3	−10	−4
High growth[a]	−12	−23	−16	−2	−10	−10	−4
Change in direct consumption							
Low growth	−39	−6	−1	−2	−20	−34	3
High growth	−31	−6	−1	1	−8	−21	19
Change in indirect consumption							
Low growth	. . .	−33	−16	. . .	. . .	. . .	. . .
High growth	. . .	−24	−6	. . .	. . .	. . .	. . .
Change in production							
Low growth	. . .	14	14	−26	−16	−10	−10
High growth	. . .	27	24	−12	6	7	8
				(million metric tons)			
Change in net exports[b]							
Low growth	0.4	16.8	15.1	−0.7	3.4	1.5	−0.6
High growth	0.3	21.4	16.4	−0.5	8.2	1.4	−0.7
Net export volume							
Low growth	−0.6	18.7	12.9	−4.3	−3.2	−0.3	−1.5
High growth	−0.7	22.8	14.5	−4.1	1.7	0.3	−1.6
U.S. net export volume							
Low growth	3.5	48.2	141.0	−0.1	15.4	1.1	0.0
High growth	3.5	47.5	141.0	−0.1	13.9	1.1	−0.5

Source: Results from the analysis using the model described in Appendix 1.

Notes: These results examine the incremental effect of food market liberalization in the Balkans and the former Soviet Union. The reference simulation in this case includes unilateral reform and expansion of the European Union to include the European Free Trade Association countries, as well as extension of the Common Agricultural Policy to cover EE-3 farmers. The EE-3 includes the former Czechoslovakia, Hungary, and Poland. Corresponding results for the Balkans and the other former Soviet Union states are given in Table 5 of the data supplement to this report, available on request from the International Food Policy Research Institute.

[a]The low- and high-growth scenarios here refer to the EE-3 (in the reference simulation used), the Balkans, and the former Soviet Union.

[b]Where positive, a change in net exports indicates increased exports or a reduction in net imports, depending on which prevailed in the reference case.

substantial net surplus of grains. This result is striking, given that the region as a whole has been a net importer of grains for half a century. Nevertheless, Russia's predicted net grain exports in 2000 still amount to less than a fifth of those predicted for the United States in that year.[36] In any case, if the governments of the former Soviet Union continue to keep domestic grain prices low they may never emerge.

---

[36]The prediction that liberalization in the former Soviet Union will lead to net grain exports is robust to variations in assumptions about prereform distortions, the extent of queuing waste associated with consumer subsidies (Chapter 3), and the potential for productivity improvements in food production. It stems from high rates of prereform protection of livestock farms and subsidies to grain consumption. There is little dispute that this reflects the pattern of prereform distortions.

The international price effects of reform in the Balkans and the former Soviet Union, with high growth, are charted over the two decade phase-in period in Figure 8. Note, first, that downward pressure is applied to grain prices very early on. This is the result of the assumption that the reforms are phased over the period 1991-95. In spite of substantial nominal increases, grain prices in Russia remained quite low compared with import parity through early 1993 (Konovalov et al. 1993), which indicates that liberalization is proceeding more slowly than is simulated here. Second, as in the EE-3, these international market effects stabilize as the regional economy recovers from the transitional slump. Finally, the long-term effect of liberalization in the Balkans and the former Soviet Union, combined with high recovery growth, is a regional net surplus of dairy products. This is primarily due to the assumption that the productivity of the dairy industry in the former Soviet Union improves by 50 percent (Table 10). For reasons discussed in Chapter 3, it is difficult to imagine such a catch-up not occurring. It is likely, however, that natural barriers (quality or health constraints) or trade distortions in the rest of Europe will ultimately restrict these net exports.

The consequences of reform in all the postsocialist economies for overall self-sufficiency in GLS and net food export earnings are summarized in Table 16. Reform in the EE-3 and the former Soviet Union enhances the terms of trade of the Balkan states, since they were previously net importers of wheat, the price of which falls substantially. Their net food export earnings therefore increase, as does their overall level of self-sufficiency, both in the low-growth and the high-growth scenarios. For the former Soviet republics, the direction of effects on these two measures depends on exogenous income and productivity growth. The general pattern is one of in-

Figure 8— Incremental world price changes, former Soviet Union, 1990-2010

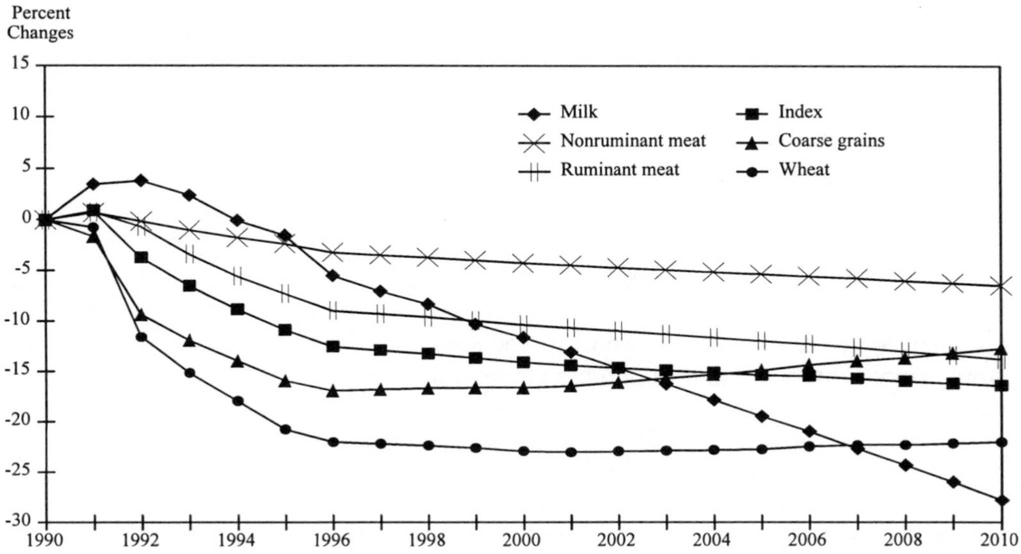

Source: Results from the analysis using the model described in Appendix 1.

Table 16— Incremental effects on self-sufficiency and net food export earnings of economic change and food price reform in EE-3, the Balkans, and the former Soviet Union, 2000

Economic Group or Country	Food Self-Sufficiency[a]			Net Food Export Earnings[a]		
	No Reform[b]	Low Growth[c]	High Growth[c]	No Reform[b]	Low Growth[c]	High Growth[c]
	(percent)			(1990 US$ billion)		
EE-3	102	123	130	0.5	5.9	8.0
Balkans	103	123	128	0.6	3.7	4.7
Russia	87	101	104	−7.3	0.4	2.0
Ukraine	115	133	137	3.2	5.0	6.2
Baltic states	147	185	183	1.7	1.9	2.4
Western republics	76	91	95	−2.9	−0.9	−0.6
Kazakhstan	130	146	160	1.9	2.2	3.1
Central Asia	37	41	44	−6.3	−4.8	−4.5
Total Eastern Europe and former Soviet Union	94	111	116	−8.6	16.6	21.3
United States	131	127	126	33.3	28.3	25.7

Source: Results from the analysis using the model described in Appendix 1.

Notes: The EE-3 countries are the former Czechoslovakia, Hungary, and Poland. These results examine the incremental effect of food market liberalization in the Balkans and the former Soviet Union. The reference simulation in this case includes unilateral reform in the European Union and expansion of the European Union to include the countries of the European Free Trade Association. See Table 9 for a listing of countries in each group.

[a]Food includes grain, livestock products, and sugar.

[b]The "no reform" values are for 2000 and are drawn from the revised reference simulation, explained above.

[c]The low- and high-growth scenarios here refer to the EE-3, the Balkans, and former Soviet Union.

creased self-sufficiency and lower net food import costs (or higher net food export earnings) both of which are stronger in the high-growth case. For all the postsocialist economies taken together, these reform scenarios yield self-sufficiency in food on average and net export earnings by 2000 of between 50 and 80 percent of those predicted for the United States.

International Price Effects of All European Reforms

In the preceding discussion, each new policy reform was compared with the aggregate of those that preceded it. Here, two simulations that incorporate the complete set of reforms thus far considered are compared with the original reference simulation (which assumes economic stagnation in the postsocialist countries). The extent to which reforms in Western Europe might be offset by the reforms in the postsocialist economies can then be clarified. Consider first the low-growth reform case, recalling that higher food prices followed unilateral reforms in the European Union and its expansion to include EFTA (Figure 6). The adoption of a CAP-like policy in the EE-3 was seen to neutralize these price changes by at least half (Figure 7). Liberalization in the Balkans and the former Soviet Union reinforces the external effects of EE-3 reform but the magnitude is greater (Figure 8).

It is just possible that these various reforms, carried out simultaneously, might offset each other and have little net effect on international food trade outside Europe. This would be true, for example, if the food market liberalization in the former Soviet Union were introduced more slowly than is assumed here and if it were ultimately incomplete. In the crude characterizations simulated here, however, the international effects of liberalization in the Balkans and the former Soviet Union stand out. In comparing the original reference simulation with reform throughout Europe and the former Soviet Union in the high-growth scenario, the net effect is lower international food prices, particularly of grains and eventually of dairy products (Figure 9). The corresponding price changes in 2000 are presented numerically in Table 17. From this it is evident that the potential shift toward excess food supply in the postsocialist economies has about twice the effect on international prices as the predicted shift toward excess food demand in Western Europe.

Sensitivity to Key Assumptions

By ruling out unlikely developments at the farm and household level, one hopes to use quantitative analysis to restrict the range of events in aggregate. Inevitably, uncertainties judged to be insurmountable necessitate the repetition of the analysis in multiple scenarios. Lesser uncertainties, on which some prior information or even intuition can be brought to bear, can be examined for each scenario in sensitivity

Figure 9— Aggregate world price changes as a result of reforms, 1990-2010

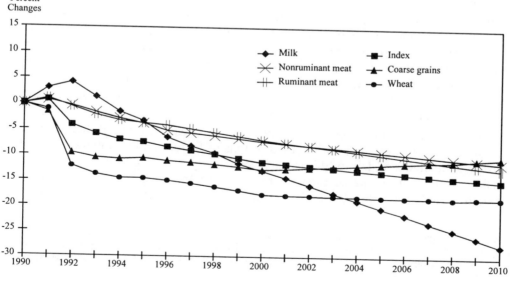

Source: Results from the analysis using the model described in Appendix 1.

Table 17—Collective effects of reforms and economic change in Europe and the former Soviet Union on international food prices, 2000

Commodity	Percent Change		
	Western European Reforms	Combined European and Former Soviet Union Reforms, Low Growth	Combined European and Former Soviet Union Reforms, High Growth
Food price index	7.0	−8.0	−11.0
Rice	5.0	−7.0	−9.0
Wheat	10.0	−13.0	−18.0
Coarse grains	7.0	−9.0	−13.0
Sugar	2.0	−0.3	−2.0
Dairy products	3.0	−5.0	−11.0
Ruminant meats	7.0	−4.0	−7.0
Nonruminant meats	−0.3	−5.0	−7.0

Source: Results from the analysis using the model described in Appendix 1.
Notes: The food prices included are for grains, livestock products, and sugar. The first column gives the effects of Western European reform, assuming that the other European and former Soviet Union economies remain stagnant in the 1990s. The last two columns give the effects of economic change and reforms throughout Europe.

analysis.[37] Here this is achieved by repeating the simulations discussed previously, in each case varying the assumptions for which the literature or experience provide scant support. The results are then summarized in the form of the elasticity of sensitivity, which is the ratio of the proportional change in a key result (the change in an international price or a self-sufficiency level) and the corresponding proportional change in an underlying assumption (the assumed magnitude of consumer incentive price premia, for example).

Three such assumptions are examined in this way. All are concerned with the interpretation of the estimates of prereform incentive distortions in the former Soviet Union, discussed in Chapter 3. The first is the generic change in all relative food prices that occurs as a consequence of changes of policy elsewhere in the economy. The core analysis assumes that the prereform subsidy equivalents were estimated at an overvalued exchange rate (or at least at a rate likely to be unrepresentative in the foreseeable future), and hence that policy discrimination against agriculture was greater in the late 1980s than suggested by those estimates. So the first sensitivity analysis varies the size of this generic change.

The second concerns uncertainty about the true extent of food production subsidies in the prereform period. Indirect distortions of factor and input markets and the subsidy equivalents of debt write-offs are imperfectly accounted for in the producer subsidy equivalent estimates used. In the late 1980s, the debt write-offs were a substantial and increasing form of assistance to the food sector.[38] To account for

---

[37]Still lesser uncertainties (risks in the Knightian sense) are readily incorporated into the analysis, appearing in the results as forecast error bands or confidence intervals. Given the rich spread of results from both the scenarios and the sensitivity analysis, simplicity of presentation dictates that these intervals be suppressed in this case.

[38]See the discussion on this topic in Chapter 3.

48

these in the core analysis, each prereform relative producer price in the former Soviet Union is raised by an arbitrary 50 percent of its corresponding border price (Table 6). The second sensitivity analysis varies the size of this adjustment.

The third is the assumption that there are incentive price premia over the official prereform state shop food prices. In the core analysis, these premia are estimated based on the gap between private market and state shop prices. Queuing at heavily subsidized state shops is represented, following Morduch, Brooks, and Urinson 1994, as a private market with lump-sum transfers to those whose opportunity cost of queuing time is low or who receive food at state shop prices through their employers. But the premia for sugar and livestock products are extraordinarily large (on the order of 300 percent for livestock products). So the third sensitivity analysis varies the prereform consumer incentive prices of sugar and livestock products.

The sensitivity of shifts in international food prices to these variations is quantified in Table 18. International food prices are comparatively insensitive to variations in across-the-board production subsidies, taken alone. They are similarly insensitive to consumer price premia when these are also varied in isolation. More sensitivity would be expected from simultaneous variations in prereform producer and consumer incentives. And, for this reason, the generic changes in all prereform incentive prices

Table 18— Elasticities of sensitivity to key assumptions about incentives, 2000

	Sensitivity of the International Price of							
Assumption	Rice	Wheat	Coarse Grain	Sugar	Dairy Products	Ruminant Meat	Non-ruminant Meat	GLS Index
Generic price effects of nonfood in the former Soviet Union reforms[a]								
Low growth	−0.08	−0.12	−0.10	−0.10	−0.24	−0.16	−0.08	−0.13
High growth	−0.08	−0.14	−0.12	−0.08	−0.20	−0.18	−0.08	−0.13
Excluded former Soviet Union production subsidies[b]								
Low growth	0.04	0.06	0.06	0.04	0.08	0.06	0.04	0.06
High growth	0.06	0.06	0.06	0.02	0.08	0.05	0.04	0.07
Former Soviet Union consumer incentive price premia[c]								
Low growth	0.02	0.01	0.03	0.03	0.13	0.06	0.02	0.05
High growth	0.02	0.01	0.02	0.05	0.12	0.04	0.03	0.04

Source: Results from the analysis using the model described in Appendix 1.
Notes: Elasticities of sensitivity give the proportional change in some result (an international price level in this case) that occurs following a unit proportional change in a parameter.
[a]The generic increase in all relative prices of grain, livestock products, and sugar (GLS) occurs as a consequence, for example, of a real devaluation and its effects on the overall terms of trade facing the food sector. The core analysis assumes a 50 percent improvement. The elasticities indicate that a further 10 percent generic increase would cause the postreform GLS index, for example, to be smaller by 1.3 percent in the low-growth case.
[b]Among the excluded subsidies are some border input price distortions and debt write-offs. The core analysis assumes these raised prereform nominal protection rates by 50 percent. The elasticities indicate that, were these to have been worth a further 10 percent of the border price, the postreform GLS index, for example, would become larger by 0.6 percent in the low-growth case.
[c]Prereform consumer incentive price premia are imposed over the state shop prices of sugar, milk, and meats. The elasticities indicate that, had these premia been larger by 10 percent of the border price, the postreform GLS index would be larger by 0.5 percent in the low-growth case.

indeed yield higher elasticities of sensitivity in the reform scenarios.[39] Postreform international dairy product and ruminant meat prices are apparently most sensitive to generic errors in estimates of prereform incentive distortions. This is not surprising given the comparatively large shares of these commodities in the total value of GLS consumption and production in the postsocialist countries.

The corresponding sensitivity to the above variations of aggregate food self-sufficiency in both the postsocialist countries and developing countries as a group is indicated in Table 19. According to the estimates, postreform self-sufficiency in the postsocialist economies would be higher by about a quarter if prereform exchange rate overvaluation were larger than postulated so that reform would bring an additional generic doubling of incentive producer and consumer prices. The other elasticities of sensitivity are smaller for the same reasons that international prices are

Table 19— Elasticities of sensitivity of postreform self-sufficiency levels to key assumptions, 2000

	Sensitivity of Food Self-Sufficiency in		
Assumption	Russia	All Postsocialist Economies	All Developing Economies
Generic price effects of nonfood former Soviet Union policies[a]			
Low growth	0.26	0.22	−0.04
High growth	0.28	0.24	−0.04
Excluded former Soviet Union production subsidies[b]			
Low growth	−0.10	−0.10	0.0
High growth	−0.12	−0.12	0.02
Former Soviet Union consumer incentive price premia[c]			
Low growth	−0.12	−0.10	0.02
High growth	−0.12	−0.12	0.02

Source: Results from the analysis using the model described in Appendix 1.
Note: Elasticities of sensitivity give the proportional change in some result (an international price level in this case) that occurs following a unit proportional change in a parameter.
[a]The generic increase in all relative grain, livestock, and sugar (GLS) prices occurs as a consequence, for example, of a real devaluation and its effects on the overall terms of trade facing the food sector. The core analysis assumes a 50 percent improvement. The elasticities indicate that a further 10 percent generic increase would cause Russian postreform self-sufficiency, for example, to be larger by 2.6 percent of consumption value.
[b]Indirect subsidies include some border input price distortions and debt write-offs. The core analysis assumes these raised prereform nominal protection rates by 50 percent. The elasticities indicate that, were these to have been worth a further 10 percent of the border price, Russian postreform self-sufficiency, for example, would become smaller by 1 percent of consumption value.
[c]Prereform consumer incentive price premia are imposed over the state shop prices of sugar, milk, and meats. The elasticities indicate that, had these premia been larger by 10 percent of the border price, Russian postreform self-sufficiency, for example, would be smaller by 1.2 percent of consumption value.

---

[39]They are, in fact, larger than the sum of the other two corresponding elasticities. This is expected, given that the consumer price premia are applied only to sugar and livestock products. But the difference may also be enhanced by nonlinearity.

lower. The average level of food self-sufficiency of developing countries as a group is understandably less sensitive to price policy in the former Soviet Union than are results specific to that region. Nevertheless, a generic doubling of postreform incentive prices in the Balkans and the former Soviet Union would reduce average self-sufficiency in developing countries by 4 percentage points.

As crude measures of margins of error, these elasticities of sensitivity are tolerable for a study of this type. They are primarily used as a means of transforming key results presented earlier in the chapter to account for the quite likely event that one or more of the assumptions of the core analysis is eventually found to be in error and the direction and magnitude of the error is known. In this vein, one application stems from the discussion of the eventual shape of the hypothetically market-oriented postsocialist economies in Chapter 4. As Anderson (1992; 1993) indicates, agriculture's domestic terms of trade will depend on the evolution of comparative advantage in these economies and, in the medium term, on which sector responds first to the reformed incentives.

The core analysis presented here is consistent with the presumption that the agricultural sector will be the first to respond. Considering, however, the possibility that the former Soviet Union will emerge from the transitional slump with an export boom in the minerals and energy sector, such a boom would tend to draw factors and inputs from agriculture, raising their prices. This could be represented in the above analysis by higher prereform relative producer incentive prices (lower prereform as compared with postreform production costs). A rise in variable costs of, say, 50 percent could be represented as a decline in incentive prices of about a third (if commercial inputs and mobile factors absorb two-thirds of the farm budget). The postreform international GLS price index would be higher by 2 percent and self-sufficiency in postsocialist economies lower by 3 percent (Table 18). But this would be only half the story. Such a boom would also cause the real exchange rate to appreciate. Saying that this appreciation is by 20 percent and that the proportion of nontradables in the agricultural input and final consumption baskets is such that this is equivalent to a reduction in producer and consumer incentive prices of about 10 percent, then the postreform international GLS index would be lower by an additional 1.3 percent, for a total of 3.3 percent, and the level of postsocialist food self-sufficiency would be lower by an additional 2 percent, for a total of 5 percent. Although these hypothetical changes are substantial, they are considerably less than what would be required to reverse the conclusions of the core analysis, which are that food surpluses are likely in the postsocialist economies, particularly if the former Soviet Union proceeds with full liberalization, and that the global effect of their reforms will be lower international food prices. This is true even in the low-growth reform scenario where the analysis predicts the least reduction in international food prices and, correspondingly, the least increase in postsocialist food self-sufficiency.

6

IMPLICATIONS FOR OTHER DEVELOPING COUNTRIES

The analysis of the previous chapter concludes that the most likely consequence of the unilateral reforms in Western Europe, combined with the successful conversion of Eastern Europe and the former Soviet Union to market economies, is lower international food prices. This result is summarized in Figure 10, which shows only the indices of international food prices in each of the three scenarios. In the first decade of the new millennium, the price of food could be reduced by 4-16 percent.

The ultimate effect of European and postsocialist economic change on international prices is most likely to lie between these two extremes. This is because, on the one hand, the low-growth scenario is pessimistic about productivity gains from economic reform in the postsocialist economies. On the other hand, the high-growth scenario is optimistic about the extent to which economic reforms of the former Soviet Union will ultimately liberalize internal food markets. Moreover, the average price declines in the high-growth scenario, in part because of a substantial increase in dairy product exports from the former Soviet Union. Most likely, this flow would be stemmed by natural barriers not accounted for in the foregoing analysis or internal distortions such as the production quotas present in Europe. And finally, a boom in manufactured exports from part of the region, such as the EE-3, or in minerals

Figure 10—Indices of world food prices for three scenarios, 1990-2010

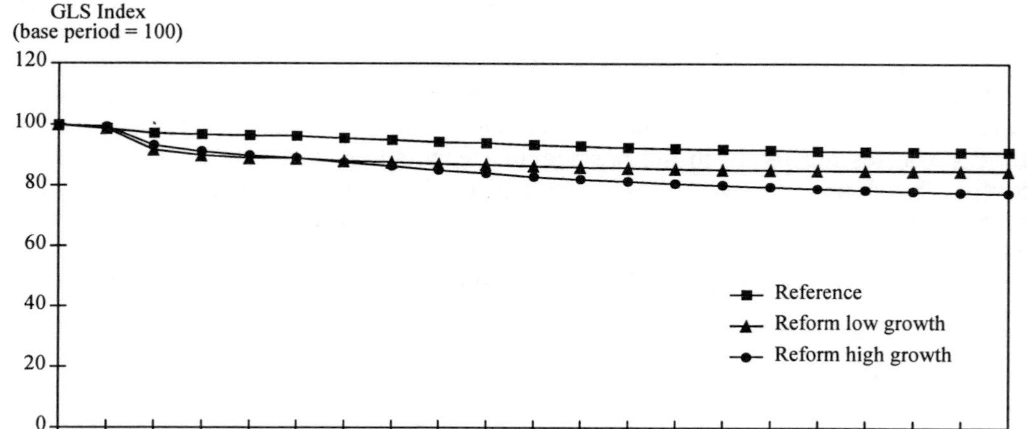

Source: Results from the analysis using the model described in Appendix 1.
Note: GLS is grains, livestock products, and sugar.

exports from the former Soviet Union could slow down the region's agricultural export growth and offset the predicted shift in the global terms of trade.

It should also be noted that the foregoing analysis examines the effects on world markets of economic changes only in Europe and the former Soviet Union. It ignores the specific agreements emerging from the now completed Uruguay Round of trade negotiations, which, although they will add little to the extent of Europe's reforms, will also reduce agricultural distortions outside Europe. The Agreement on Agriculture (GATT 1994) requires reductions in support in all signatory countries, including developing countries. But the effects on the international terms of trade of reducing the most substantial remaining protection, mainly in North America and Japan, will not be large (see Tyers and Anderson 1992, Table 6.2). In the United States, the trade effects of its protection have been buffered by quantity controls. In Japan, while rice protection has been very high, similarly high beef protection has boosted feed demand and hence other cereal imports. Indeed, the tendency of the Uruguay Round agreement to make international food prices higher than they would otherwise be is mitigated by its extension to many developing countries whose policy regimes have discriminated against their agricultural sectors. Agreed reforms in these countries could raise their food production sufficiently to reduce the GLS index of international food prices by several percent (Tyers 1994). Moreover, some developing countries have recently embarked on unilateral reforms of their own, further improving incentives for food production at home (Valdés 1992a). Thus, the effects of the industrial-country reforms not considered in the above analysis are likely to be offset by reforms in developing countries that had previously taxed agriculture.

If the most likely outcome is a decline in relative international food prices, is this advantageous for developing countries? Answers to this question are not straightforward. Even if all developing countries were net importers of food, it would not be possible to conclude with certainty that they would be net beneficiaries. This is because most of them, and particularly the poorest, still have highly distorted economies.

The Simple Welfare Economics of a Shift in the Terms of Trade

Let us begin with the crude assumption that a single welfare measure is possible for all households in a developing country. In essence, this implies that preferences are identical and homothetic, and hence measures of individual household welfare can be aggregated across the country as a whole without bias. Then, the net welfare effect of a change in the external terms of trade (in particular, a fall in relative food prices) depends on whether the domestic economy is distorted and whether the change in the terms of trade is transmitted to the domestic market. It therefore depends on both the protection and the insulating components of the policies affecting each tradable goods sector (Tyers and Falvey 1989). The following abstraction illustrates this point. Agricultural trade is most often distorted using a variety of nontariff barriers, including state trading,[40] with the explicit objective of insulating

---

[40]State trading is usually characterized by the mandated monopolization of all trade in a focus commodity, such as a food grain, by a parastatal agency. Examples in developing countries are the Food Corporation of India and the National Logistics Agency (BULOG) in Indonesia.

domestic markets at some desired price level. Imagine that there is a change, dP, in the vector of border prices, P. Then the eventual changes in domestic consumer, c, and producer prices, p, are

$$dp^C = \phi^C \, dP,\tag{1}$$

and

$$dp^P = \phi^P \, dP,\tag{2}$$

where ϕ^c and ϕ^P are vector rates of price transmission for consumer and producer prices respectively.[41] If these are set to zero, insulation is complete and no border price changes are transmitted. If they are set to unity, border price changes are fully transmitted. Now add the following linear approximations to the domestic demand and supply curves for each traded commodity k.

$$D^k = D_F^k + \sum_{j=1}^{J} D_j^k (p_j^C - P_j),\tag{3}$$

and

$$S^k = S_F^k + \sum_{j=1}^{J} S_j^k (p_j^P - P_j),\tag{4}$$

where D_F denotes the home compensated demand and S_F the corresponding net supply levels of commodity k that would prevail at border prices (free trade). The terms $(p^C - P)$ and $(p^P - P)$ indicate the degree to which the domestic consumer and producer prices are distorted.

If a change, dP_k, occurs in the international price of commodity k, then the reasoning of Tyers and Falvey can be used to derive the following simple expression for the change in domestic economic welfare dW:

$$dW = \sum_{k=1}^{J} \left[(\phi_k^C - 1) \sum_{j=1}^{J} (p_j^C - P_j) D_k^j - (\phi_k^P - 1) \sum_{j=1}^{J} (p_j^P - P_j) S_k^j - (D_F^k - S_F^k) \right] dP_k.\tag{5}$$

This equation illustrates the importance of the hypothetical undistorted net trade position of the country in evaluating the welfare effects of a change in the terms of trade. The last term gives this effect. It is the marginal change in the net earnings from trade *measured at undistorted trade volumes*. If there are no distortions, then the expression collapses to this term. If there are distortions, but these take the form, for example, of tariffs that fully transmit border price changes, then $\phi^C = \phi^P = 1$ and the welfare effect is still determined by the third term. If, however, the economy is both distorted and insulated (as is most common), then the other terms enter.

In the extreme case where the insulation is total ($\phi^C = \phi^P = 0$), then the equation reduces to

$$dW = \sum_{k=1}^{J} - (D_k - S_k) \, dP_k,\tag{6}$$

[41]The rates of price transmission used here are the linear counterparts of the elasticities of price transmission used in the Tyers-Anderson model, presented in Appendix 1 and documented in Tyers and Anderson 1992 and in the supplement to this report, available on request from the International Food Policy Research Institute.

where, from equation (2), D_k and S_k are the distorted domestic demands and supplies. Thus, if the insulation is total, then the welfare effect of a marginal shift in the terms of trade is approximately equal to the change in net export earnings *measured at the distorted trade volumes*. Considering that protection frequently reverses the direction of net trade, if the distorted volumes are always used in welfare approximations, then the results can be in error not only in magnitude but also in sign.

The case of a developing country facing a decline in its food import price can be summarized as follows. If the decline is fully transmitted and the economy would be a net importer of food in the absence of distortions, then welfare improves. If it is not, then the effect depends on whether the economy remains a net importer after the distortions are taken into account. If so, then welfare improves. But the country may be taxing its food agriculture so heavily that the direction of trade is reversed from net exports to net imports, a not uncommon circumstance.[42] In that case, even though the country is currently a net food importer, the decline in the food import price causes a net reduction in welfare.

To complicate matters, the poor in developing countries, who live primarily in rural areas (World Bank et al. 1990), may well have preferences that are different from those generally better-off urban households. Certainly, their marginal utilities of income must be greater. Since their welfare depends on the general level of economic activity in rural areas, they would be better off with higher food prices or at least higher agricultural product prices. Some indication of this is evident from simple trade models. In the Heckscher-Ohlin world of two goods (food, which is labor-intensive, and manufactures) and two factors (labor and capital, including land), a decline in the external price of food yields a decline in the domestic wage that is larger than that in the food price. Laborers are clearly worse off. When the model is complicated by the inclusion of land as a factor specific to agriculture, the picture is clouded and the result depends on worker household expenditure shares on food, on elasticities of substitution between labor and land in agriculture, and between labor and capital in manufacturing (Scott 1992). Reasonable parameter values nevertheless yield a net decline in the real wage. This decline is only exacerbated by the inclusion in the model of higher manufacturing wages and Harris-Todaro unemployment.

Measures of the Impact on Other Developing Countries

A variety of measures of the welfare effects of lower international food prices on developing countries are listed in Table 20. All the results presented compare the original reference simulation with European and former Soviet Union reforms with a high-growth recovery in the postsocialist economies. These include partial equilibrium approximations of net welfare effects, which add up the income equivalents of price changes for consumers, farmers, and the government. These are particularly crude when applied to developing countries because they do not properly account for indirect effects on agriculture of distortions elsewhere in the economy. Since these indirect effects are generally biased against agriculture, this measure tends to underestimate gains from a terms-of-trade change that favors agriculture.

---

[42]See Krueger, Schiff, and Valdés 1988; Schiff and Valdés 1992; and a summary in Valdés 1992b for examples of particularly heavy net taxation of agriculture in developing countries.

Table 20—Measures of the welfare effects on other developing countries of lower international food prices due to European and former Soviet Union reforms, combined with strong associated growth in Eastern Europe and the former Soviet Union, 2000

Country	Net Change in			Food Self-Sufficiency[a]	
	Economic Welfare[b]	Producer Surplus	Net Food Export Earnings[c]	Reference	Under High Growth Due to Reforms in Europe and the Former Soviet Union
	(US$ billion)			(percent)	
China	1.7	−4.4	−0.1	89	88
Indonesia	0.3	−0.6	−0.2	85	83
Philippines	0.1	−0.1	0.0	92	92
Thailand	−0.1	−0.3	−0.3	120	116
Bangladesh	0.2	−0.5	−0.2	85	82
India	0.4	−2.8	−1.2	96	94
Pakistan	0.3	−0.4	−0.1	81	78
Other Asian countries	0.2	−1.0	−0.3	86	84
Argentina	−0.4	−0.6	−1.0	116	110
Brazil	0.7	−2.3	−1.2	95	91
Mexico	0.7	−1.0	−0.1	84	81
Other Latin American countries	0.3	−0.9	−0.7	90	86
Egypt	0.6	−0.1	0.2	64	64
Nigeria	0.2	−0.2	−0.1	74	70
Other Sub-Saharan African countries	0.2	−0.6	−0.6	86	82
South Africa	0.2	−0.5	−0.4	94	88
Other North African and Middle Eastern countries	1.6	−0.6	−0.8	75	75
Total	7.2	−16.9	−7.1	90	88

Source: Results from the analysis using the model described in Appendix 1.

Notes: This table compares the original reference scenario, in which economic stagnation after 1990 is assumed in Eastern Europe and the former Soviet Union, with the high-growth reform scenario.

[a]Food self-sufficiency is measured as the value at base-period international prices of food (grains, livestock products, and sugar) production, divided by the corresponding value of consumption and expressed in percentages.

[b]The income equivalent of producer and consumer price changes is measured as the sum of the equivalent variation in consumer income, the change in producer surplus, and any change in average stock profits (see R. Tyers and K. Anderson, *Disarray in World Food Markets: A Quantitative Assessment* [Cambridge, U.K.: Cambridge University Press, 1992], Appendix 1). In the context of the partial equilibrium Tyers-Anderson model, where indirect distortions affecting agriculture are incompletely accounted for, these measures are an approximation at best when applied to developing countries.

To capture some of the effects of a food price change on rural economic activity, estimates of the change in the food surplus at the farm level in developing countries are also included. Also included in the table are the corresponding changes in food self-sufficiency and net export earnings from food trade. Ignoring differences between the poor and other groups in developing countries, the results suggest that most developing countries would be marginal net beneficiaries of the decline in world food prices. The only exceptions are the substantial net food exporters, Thailand and Argentina. But the net effects are small and would very likely be reversed were the indirect distortions against agriculture taken into account.

There are, in fact, at least two reasons for the lack of robust results in the first column of Table 20. First, the underlying estimates of incentive distortions in developing countries capture only incompletely the indirect effects, usually adverse to agriculture, of exchange controls and manufacturing protection.[43] Were this discrimination against agriculture fully captured in the analysis, net food-exporting developing countries would export more and net importers would import less. Even if no country reverses the direction of its food trade, developing countries as a group could become net food exporters and hence, in aggregate, their net welfare would be impaired by the lower international food prices. Second, while investment in improvements in food productivity are expected to increase in Eastern Europe and the former Soviet Union, lower world food prices could reduce this type of investment in agriculture in developing countries (Tyers and Anderson 1992, chap.4.4). Since the 1950s, cereal productivity growth has been higher in developing countries than elsewhere in the world (Tyers and Anderson 1992, Table 1.5). The continuation of this trend would in time reduce their net dependence on food imports and hence increase the likelihood that, in aggregate, they would lose from a decline in international food prices.

As for the other measures, cheaper food is uniformly deleterious to rural interests, as the producer surplus estimates in Table 20 confirm. This is a more likely index of the interests of the poor in developing countries. Food self-sufficiency in developing countries as a group declines only slightly, however. Changes in net food export earnings also depend on the extent to which domestic markets are insulated from external changes. If no price change is transmitted to the domestic market, then a net importer enjoys a decline in the net cost of food imports (registering as a positive entry in the third column of Table 20). If the change is fully transmitted, the volume of net food imports increases and this may offset the valuation effect of lower prices. Clearly, the valuation effect is dominant in Egypt, while the volume effects appear to dominate elsewhere.

Importantly, the net effect of the change in the terms of trade on the balance of payments of developing countries is small. With the possible exception of India, it does not suggest any difficulty associated with the financing of added food imports. The smallness of this result is in stark contrast with the effect on their balance of payments of the increased demand for capital in Eastern Europe and the former Soviet Union. While not all developing countries are net importers of staple foods, all are net importers of capital. Moreover, these capital imports are essential to continued economic growth. The discussion in Chapter 4, which draws on studies by Collins and Rodrik (1991) and McKibbin (1991), concludes that there could be a decline in net transfers to developing countries of at least US$30 billion per year. This would be combined with the crowding out of investment and hence slower output growth in industrial countries (except Germany) and slower growth in demand for the exports of most developing countries. Such changes will clearly dominate any effects transmitted directly through international trade in food products.

---

[43]The estimates of incentive distortions in developing countries that are used in the model are listed in the supplement to this report. These are based primarily on PSE and CSE estimates by Webb, Lopez, and Penn (1990) and those by Sullivan et al. (1992). They exclude some of the indirect distortions adverse to agriculture that were calculated for 18 developing countries by Krueger, Schiff, and Valdés (1988) and by Schiff and Valdés (1992).

7

CONCLUSIONS

In Eastern Europe and the former Soviet Union, virtually all of the constituent republics have embarked upon ambitious programs of economic reform directed toward establishing market economies on the Western European model. With the collapse of the Soviet Union, these republics lost most of their intraregional export markets, while trading opportunities in the West were opening only slowly. As many of the republics sought to gain economic independence from Moscow, the centrally administered infrastructure of the Soviet Union became ineffective. For many products, however, there has not yet been time to replace it with private, or at least local, marketing channels. Ironically, given that it was the pressures for new economic growth that brought them about, these changes, combined with local ethnic conflicts, have temporarily depleted the economies of both Eastern Europe and the former Soviet Union.

Beginning in the mid-1960s, the socialist economies centrally directed their agriculture sectors to expand meat and dairy product supplies. Agriculture was increasingly assisted in this by central governments, which, in turn, subsidized the consumption of many staple foods available through state shops. The broad pattern of incentive distortions in the region's agriculture, therefore, favored mainly livestock production on the supply side. On the demand side, although most staple foods were available at low prices through state shops, supply problems led to increasingly long queues for livestock products and the expansion of supplies of these products at comparatively high prices through unregulated private markets. Thus, by the late 1980s, cereal consumption was still subsidized while marginal consumer prices for some livestock products were near those at the border.

In combination, then, these incentive distortions raised the excess demand for cereals, which were consumed both directly and as animal feed, and reduced the excess demand for livestock products. More important to the assessment of the sector's future potential, however, is the amount of waste in distribution and processing of food products and the poor productivity achieved on farms. Wastage rates of between a quarter and a third have been reported for the main staple foods, compared with less than a tenth in Western Europe. Improvements in food processing and distribution could therefore yield substantial reductions in apparent consumption. On the production side, the central planning system's access to Western technology was limited by its poor capacity to reward foreign firms who were willing to trade technology and by the concentration of its espionage effort in the military sphere. This isolation limited access to foreign food technology advances. Cost-reducing innovation was particularly tardy on farms in the Soviet Union. Most of its food was produced on very large state and cooperative farms where management's main constituency was the farm work force. Hence, productivity improvements were often rejected or hidden to avoid subsequent increases in assigned production quotas. The result was increasing technological backwardness. With the exception of some of the states of Eastern Europe, particularly Hungary, yield comparisons suggest farm productivity now falls short of achievements in the West by between a third and a half for most cereal and livestock products.

In the short run, the collapse in aggregate economic output in Eastern Europe and the former Soviet Union will reduce purchasing power and hence the consumption of income-elastic foods such as livestock products. This, in turn, will reduce livestock herds and grain consumption. This change alone could cause a substantial reduction in net food imports and possibly a reversal in the direction of the whole region's net food trade. In the longer term, a general trend in the Eastern European and former Soviet Union economies toward a more market-oriented system with reduced incentive distortions would yield higher cereal prices relative to livestock prices and hence the possibility of net cereal exports. Although the consumption of livestock products could increase again, in practice this tendency might be offset by the availability of a more diverse range of specialty foods as in the West. Given time for improvements in the food distribution and marketing system and the achievement of technological parity, however, these economies could become substantial net exporters of most staple foods.

At the same time, changes in Western Europe should reduce assistance to its agriculture, both because of the unilateral reforms now agreed to and because agriculture in the EFTA countries has been more highly protected than in the European Union countries. Their membership in the European Union should therefore substantially reduce their agricultural assistance. Interestingly, then, while Western European food production late in the decade should be lower than it would be were no policy changes made, production in the East should (eventually) be higher. The two changes could be offsetting and hence have little net impact on international food markets.

Quantitative analysis on this point suggests that the move toward excess supply in Eastern Europe and the former Soviet Union would dominate; hence, the whole region's net food exports would tend to expand. In particular, if the model's abstraction of the region's agriculture is accurate, the unilateral reform in Western Europe, combined with the effect of EFTA membership in the European Union, would reduce Western Europe's net grain exports by more than 30 million metric tons and net beef exports by more than 2 million metric tons. By itself, such a change could cause international cereal prices to be higher by about 10 percent and beef prices higher by 7 percent. It is assumed that no substantial reform of the dairy sector is included in the unilateral reform package. Dairy farms in the original EU-12 are assumed to remain quota-constrained, while dairy protection in the EFTA will decline, which will lead to reduced production and, hence, a rise in international dairy prices. Dairy resources will shift to the production of other livestock products, causing international prices of nonruminant meats to be slightly lower. Overall, however, an index of international GLS prices is expected to be higher by about 7 percent.

The reforms in Eastern Europe are not homogeneous. The former Czechoslovakia, Hungary, and Poland are close to the European Union politically, and they have already signed Association Agreements ensuring that an increasing share of their products, including their food products, can be sold to the European Union at internal EU prices. Although these agreements offer only gradual expansion in access to EU markets, they represent the likely future policy direction for those three Eastern European countries. The full conformity of their agricultural policies with the reformed CAP, phased over two decades, would, by itself, not cause large changes in most world food markets. The exception is the dairy sector. Access to EU product prices would cause a surge in its output, which is here assumed to be constrained by quotas to a maximum of 25 percent over its 1990 level. Nevertheless, subsidized exports of milk products will rise and dairy prices in their highly insulated international market will fall. Indeed, increased excess supplies of other food products are also likely to reduce international trading prices. Reforms in this most advanced region of East and Central Europe, by themselves, would reduce the index of GLS international prices by a modest 3 percent.

Of wider interest is the effect of conformity with the CAP on government expenditures. The results suggest that the reductions in protection that would accompany EFTA membership in the European Union would bring substantial savings in CAP expenditure. If conformity with the CAP in the former Czechoslovakia, Hungary, and Poland also implies integration, at least of their agricultural sectors, the greater part of these savings would be lost by the year 2000. Moreover, full conformity is assumed to take two decades, at the end of which time substantial further CAP reforms will be needed to prevent a net expansion of its effects on country budgets.

In the Balkan states and the former Soviet Union, the trend of agricultural policy is comparatively uncertain. Economic liberalization is the stated aim of most governments in this region, although farm groups are becoming better organized and may influence policy substantially in future. The assumption in this analysis that the trend toward economic liberalization will continue accords with the perception, stemming from the experience of other reforming socialist economies, that substantial increases in value added can be generated more quickly in the agricultural sector than elsewhere, following liberalization, and that this growth helps to cushion the inevitable slump in other tradable goods sectors. These results must be interpreted with caution, however. They rest on the assumption that the former Soviet Union will eventually remove all of its distortions of agricultural incentives. Recent developments in the rural sector there suggest that, in spite of progressive changes by many of the central governments, market-oriented rural reforms have been slow to take effect.

The most prominent effect of such a liberalization in the overall region would be the anticipated change from a net cereal deficit to a net surplus of 30-50 million tons per year by the end of the decade. Taken in isolation, this would bring international grain prices down 15-20 percent. The index of GLS world prices would be correspondingly lower by 12-14 percent. Importantly, however, these changes occur during the course of the region's reforms but tend to abate as incomes grow again in the recovery period.

Comparing the reforms in Western Europe with those in the postsocialist economies, there is indeed a tendency for one to offset the other. In grain markets, the reduced excess supplies in Western Europe are matched against the greater excess supplies in the East (mainly in the former Soviet Union). In the markets for livestock products, reduced excess milk supplies in the West are matched against increased excess supplies in the three most advanced Eastern European countries and, eventually, in the former Soviet Union. The same pattern, though with smaller international price effects, occurs in the markets for meats.

Although, as the policy reforms throughout the region unfold, the effects could well turn out to be precisely offsetting, the model results suggest that the potential food surplus in the postsocialist economies, stemming from their reduced demand in the near term, eventual improvements in food productivity, and the incentive changes associated with more balanced food prices, is so large as to exceed the likely changes in the West. In two disparate scenarios embodying reforms throughout Europe and the former Soviet Union, each compared against one in which the economies (and the food markets) of Eastern Europe and the former Soviet Union stagnate, the GLS index of international prices is projected to fall between 7 and 11 percent by the end of this decade and between 7 and 15 percent by the end of the next.

Such declines in the relative prices of staple food products in international trade are unlikely to be offset by reforms agreed to in the Uruguay Round in other countries with agricultural protection. Because of quantity controls in the United States and a highly dispersed pattern of protection in Japan, European distortions have dominated the effects on the international terms of trade caused by industrial-country protection. The net effect of reforms outside Europe and the former Soviet Union—not examined explicitly in this study—is unlikely to be upward pressure on international food prices. Any reductions in agricultural protection outside Europe will be offset by reforms in developing countries, many of which are also signatories to the Uruguay Round Protocol. Most of those countries are reforming policy regimes that discriminate against their agricultural sectors.

Should they occur, these declines in relative food trading prices will hurt net food-exporting industrial countries such as Australia, Canada, New Zealand, and the United States and help industrial countries with no comparative advantage in agriculture, such as Japan. Whether or not they are desirable from the viewpoint of developing countries, however, cannot readily be generalized. This is mainly because the incentive distortions in many developing countries have traditionally discriminated against agriculture. In the absence of those distortions, more developing countries would export food than do so today. And it is the undistorted pattern of trade (the pattern of a country's comparative advantage) that determines whether or not it gains from a change in its international terms of trade. What is clear is that farmers in developing countries would lose if food could be more cheaply imported. Since the majority of the world's poor live in the rural areas of developing countries, cheaper food would mean a reduction in the economic activity from which they earn their living.

Finally, cheaper food is unlikely to be the only change observed in the rest of the world, stemming from the reforms under way in the European region. The countries of Eastern Europe will successfully export manufactures to the West, and the republics of the former Soviet Union will export minerals and energy products in addition to food. From the viewpoint of the developing countries, however, the most important impact may come through capital markets. The smallness of the projected net effect of the food price changes on their balance of payments is in stark contrast with the effect of the increased demand for capital in Eastern Europe and the former Soviet Union. There could be a decline in net transfers to developing countries of at least US$30 billion per year. This, combined with the crowding out of investment and hence slower output growth in industrial countries (except Germany), would lead to slower growth in demand for the exports of most developing countries. Such changes will clearly dominate any effects transmitted directly through international trade in food products.

APPENDIX 1:
THE WORLD FOOD TRADE MODEL

The model used in this report is an updated version of that presented in detail in Tyers and Anderson 1992, Appendix 1. The one major change in its structure concerns the use of grain as an intermediate input. The version published previously allowed only one commodity to be an input to the livestock sectors. In this version, wheat and coarse grain are substitutable in this role. This is achieved by assuming that these two grain groups have a constant elasticity of substitution in the livestock production process.

For completeness, the full model is specified here. The equations are straightforward and comparatively few in number, recognizing that each applies to all seven commodities and all 35 countries or country groups. As explained in the text, there is both a static version, which calculates a full-adjustment equilibrium in each forecast period, and a dynamic version, in which endogenous variables in any year are dependent on their values in previous years. For simplicity, the country subscript k is dropped, except where it appears in the global market-clearing equations.

Production

Production depends on first-order Nerlovian partial adjustment in exponential form. For commodity i, production has a target level, q_i^*, which depends on a price-independent trend level of production, q^T, and on any proportional departures of the prices of commodities j from their base period reference values, p_{j0}.

$$q_{it}^* = q_{it}^T \prod_{j=1}^{J} \left(\frac{p_{jt}}{p_{j0}}\right)^{b_{0ij}} \left(\frac{p_{jt-1}}{p_{j0}}\right)^{b_{1ij}} \left(\frac{p_{jt-2}}{p_{j0}}\right)^{b_{2ij}}, \tag{7}$$

where b_{tij} are supply elasticities at lag t, J is the total number of commodities (seven in this application), and q^T has the following form:

$$q_{it}^T = q_{i0}^T \left(1 - \mu_{it}^P\right) e^{g_{it}}, \tag{8}$$

where μ^P is the fraction by which land set-asides reduce output and g is the rate at which production would grow were relative output and input prices to remain constant (such growth being due to expansion and cost-reducing technical change).

Actual production approaches its target level with lagged adjustment but is shocked in each year by the proportional random disturbance ε_{it}.

$$q_{it} = q_{it}^T \left(\frac{q_{it-1}}{q_{it-1}^T}\right) \left(\frac{q_{it}^*}{q_{it}^T} \Big/ \frac{q_{it-1}}{q_{it-1}^T}\right)^{\delta_i} e^{\varepsilon_{it}}, \tag{9}$$

where the disturbance, expressed as a vector across all commodities, takes the form

$$\varepsilon_t \sim n(0, U), \tag{10}$$

and U is the variance-covariance matrix of proportional disturbances for all commodities.

The prices faced by producers, p_{jt}, are producers' prices (later superscript P) when j corresponds to the focus product or is a competing product. But they are consumers' prices (later superscript C) when j corresponds to an input, such as feedgrain.

Production behavior in the static version of the model differs from the above in that there is no partial adjustment and no random disturbance. Thus,

$$q_{it} = q_{it}^T \prod_{j=1}^{J} \left(\frac{p_{jt}}{p_{j0}} \right)^{b_{0ij} + b_{1ij} + b_{2ij}} \tag{11}$$

Consumption

Total consumption c in year t is the sum of direct consumption, c^D, and, in the cases of wheat and coarse grains, indirect consumption as animal feed, c^F.

$$c_{it} = c_{it}^D + c_{it}^F, \tag{12}$$

where direct consumption depends on proportional departures of population, N, per capita income, y, and relative consumer prices from their base period values.

$$c_{it} = c_{i0} \left(\frac{N_t}{N_0} \right) \left(\frac{y_t}{y_0} \right)^{\eta_i} \prod_{j=1}^{J} \left(\frac{p_{jt}^c}{p_{j0}^c} \right)^{a_{ij}}, \tag{13}$$

where c_{i0} is trend base-period direct consumption, η_i is the income elasticity of demand, and the a_{ij} are the own- and cross-price elasticities of demand.

The consumption of grain (wheat and coarse grain combined) as animal feed is related to the "steady state" output of each livestock product, i; q^S via an exogenous input-output coefficient, α_i; and an exogenous time-dependent feed intensity, β_{it}.

$$c_t^F = \sum_{i=1}^{J} \alpha_i \beta_{it} q_{it}^s. \tag{14}$$

The steady-state level of livestock output is formulated in the dynamic version as follows. Over-trend production is assumed to reduce livestock populations in the short run. Under-trend production builds them up. Thus, q^S is approximated by a moving average of production levels that is adjusted for short-run deviations from trend in the following way:

$$q_{it}^s = \bar{q}_{it} \left[1 + \lambda_{0i} \left(\frac{q_{it}}{\bar{q}_{it}} - 1 \right) + \lambda_{1i} \left(\frac{q_{it-1}}{\bar{q}_{it-1}} - 1 \right) + \lambda_{2i} \left(\frac{q_{it-2}}{\bar{q}_{it-2}} - 1 \right) \right]. \tag{15}$$

Adjustments depend on short-run livestock population changes. Their direction and phasing are related to the livestock output response to a change in the price of feed. The fraction of this response in the vth year is identical for wheat and coarse grain, and hence j can correspond to either commodity in

$$\lambda_{vi} = -\left(\frac{b_{vij}}{b_{0ij} + b_{1ij} + b_{2ij}}\right). \tag{16}$$

The moving average spans three years and is adjusted for exogenous production shifters as follows:

$$\bar{q}_{it} = \frac{1}{3}\left(q_{it} + q_{it-1}\frac{q_{it}^T}{q_{it-1}^T} + q_{it-2}\frac{q_{it}^T}{q_{it-2}^T}\right). \tag{17}$$

In the static version of the model, full adjustment is assumed and q^S collapses to q, so that equations 15-17 play no role.

In previous applications of the model the allocation of c^F between wheat and coarse grain was in fixed proportions (Tyers and Anderson 1992). In this application, for both the static and dynamic versions, livestock producers choose the mix of feed grains so as to minimize input cost, subject to a constant elasticity of substition aggregation function.

$$\text{Minimize } p_2^C c_2^F + p_3^C c_3^F, \tag{18}$$

subject to

$$c^F = \left(\gamma_2 c_2^{F\frac{1+\sigma}{\sigma}} + \gamma_3 c_3^{F\frac{1+\sigma}{\sigma}}\right)^{\frac{\sigma}{1+\sigma}},$$

where the subscripts $j=2$ and $j=3$ refer to wheat and coarse grain, respectively. The (constant) elasticity of substitution (defined negative) is σ and γ_2 and γ_3 are parameters calibrated from base period feed consumption shares for wheat and coarse grain. The cost-minimizing feed demands are symmetrical, that for wheat taking the form

$$c_2^F = c^F \gamma_2^{-\sigma}\left(\frac{p_2^C}{p^F}\right)^{\sigma}, \tag{19}$$

where p^F is the consolidated feedgrain price, which is

$$p^F = \left(\gamma_2^{-\sigma} p_2^{C(1+\sigma)} + \gamma_3^{-\sigma} p_3^{C(1+\sigma)}\right)^{\frac{1}{1+\sigma}}. \tag{20}$$

Closing Stocks

For each year, the closing stocks of commodity i, s_{it}, are determined as a proportion of the trend value of either production or consumption, whichever is the larger, as follows:

$$\frac{s_{it}}{z_{it}} = \pi_i\left(p_{it+1}^s - (1+r)p_{it}^s - \theta_i\frac{s_{it}}{\bar{s}}\right) + \psi_i\left(\frac{q_{it} + s_{it-1} - \bar{q}_{it} - \bar{s}_{it}}{z_{it}}\right) + \omega_i(1 + \mu_{it}^s), \tag{21}$$

where r is the rate of interest, θ_i is the marginal cost of storage of commodity i (when stocks are at a trend level), and μ^s is the fraction by which the mean level of stocks as a proportion of the trend quantity produced or consumed is induced to depart from its base period value as a consequence of government-held stocks. The first term is the marginal expected profit from stockholding, the second is a quantity trigger, and the third is an exogenous constant. Trend value is defined as

$$z_{it} = \frac{\overline{q}_{it}, \quad \overline{q}_{it} > \overline{c}_{it}}{\overline{c}_{it}, \quad \overline{q}_{it} < \overline{c}_{it}}. \tag{22}$$

The trend level of consumption, $\overline{c}_{it}$, is a three-year moving average, adjusted for exogenous trends as for production in equation (17). A similar construction is used for the trend of stocks, s_{it}. The stockholder price is the domestic consumer price, p^C, where that price yielded the better fit in the original estimation of equation (21), as discussed in Tyers (1984). Alternatively, it is the border price, P^B reflecting instances where the home market is so insulated that stocks tend to be held only by agencies licensed to trade the commodity internationally. Its expected value in $t+1$ is a four-year moving average of past prices.

In the static version of the model, the first two terms of equation (21) collapse to zero and stocks are set at an exogenous proportion of either production or consumption.

Price Policy

Domestic prices are related to border prices by price transmission equations. These represent both the pure protection and the insulating (stabilizing) components of agricultural and commodity trade policy. Like the production equations, they take the exponential lagged adjustment form. Separate equations are specified for consumer prices and producer prices, but the formulation in each case is identical. Here it is presented in reduced form for the case of the consumer price:

$$p_{it}^C = \rho_{it}^C \, \overline{P}_{i0}^B \left(\frac{p_{it-1}^C}{\rho_{it-1}^C} \, \overline{P}_{i0}^B\right)^{\left(1 - \frac{\phi_{it}^{CSR}}{\phi_{it}^{CLR}}\right)} \left(\frac{P_{it}^B}{\overline{P}_{i0}^B}\right)^{\phi_{it}^{CSR}} \tag{23}$$

where ρ^C is the target nominal protection coefficient for consumers ($1 + \tau^C$, where τ^C is the ad valorem tariff equivalent sought by government), ϕ^{CSR} is the same-year elasticity of price transmission, and ϕ^{CLR} is the long-run elasticity of price transmission. Each of these parameters can vary through time exogenously. The corresponding expression for the producer price is identical in form. Its parameters are the producer price policy counterparts ρ^P, ϕ^{PSR}, and ϕ^{PLR}. Note that, when any one of the price transmission elasticities departs from unity and there is a change in the international price, the actual nominal protection coefficient ($1 + \tau_t$, where τ_t is the ad valorem tariff equivalent of all policies for the year t) must deviate from its target value.

In the static version of the model the consumer price transmission equation is

$$p_{it}^C = \rho_{it}^C \, \overline{P}_{i0}^B \left(\frac{P_{it}^B}{\overline{P}_{i0}^B} \right)^{\phi_{it}^{CLR}} \tag{24}$$

In both versions the border price and its base-period trend value, P_{i0}^B, are related to the international indicator price P_{it} and its base period trend value, P_{i0}, in the following way:

$$P_{it}^B = h_i \frac{P_{it}}{x_t}, \tag{25}$$

where h_i is the base-period ratio of the border price of commodity i to the chosen international indicator price for that commodity. This factor reflects country-specific quality differences, freight costs, and the pattern of concessional sales, all of which are assumed to remain constant. x_t is the exchange rate in U.S. dollars per unit of local currency. It is a parameter that can be varied exogenously to reflect changes in the relative price of product i due to changes in the real exchange rate or in price policy affecting sectors not included in the model.

Excess Demand

For country k, national excess demand for commodity i, m_{ikt}, is total consumption plus the net increase in stocks less production:

$$m_{ikt} = c_{ikt} + s_{ikt} - q_{ikt} - s_{ikt-1}. \tag{26}$$

Global Market-Clearing Condition

For global partial equilibrium in the seven commodity markets included in the model, excess demand in each should sum across countries and country groups to zero. That is,

$$\sum_{k=0}^{K} m_{ikt} = 0. \tag{27}$$

The Solution Algorithm

The objective is to derive a set of world indicator prices at which all domestic and world markets for each commodity will clear to within an acceptable tolerance. That is, global excess demand should be acceptably near to zero for each. This is achieved using an iterative Walrasian adjustment. In any year, world indicator prices are first set at their values in the previous year. The model's backward-looking expectations formulation then permits excess demands to be calculated for each of the commodities from the above equations:

$$dm_{it} = \sum_{k=1}^{K} m_{ikt} \ \forall \ i. \tag{28}$$

These global excess demands are acceptable if the following criterion is met:

where
$$dm_{it} \leq 0.0001 \, Q_{it} \quad \forall \, i, \tag{29}$$

$$Q_{it} = \sum_{k=1}^{K} q_{ikt}^T. \tag{30}$$

If one or more markets have unacceptably large global excess demands, world indicator prices are adjusted in the following matrix manipulation:

$$P_t^{New} = P_t^{Old}(1 - E^{-1}u), \tag{31}$$

where u is a vector of global excess demands, expressed as proportions of global output.

$$u = \left(\frac{dm_{it}}{Q_{it}}, \ldots, \frac{dm_{jt}}{Q_{jt}} \right), \tag{32}$$

and $E (= [e_{ij}])$ is a matrix of global excess demand elasticities. The negative sign in equation (31) is required to offset the behavioral tendency of excess demand to increase as prices decline. Here positive excess demand must induce higher market prices to bring the market into clearance. This procedure is repeated until criterion (29) is met.

Approximate values for the elements of the matrix E can be derived from the parameters of the model. Since they depend not only on domestic supply and demand elasticities but also on policy parameters, and most especially on the price transmission elasticities, the efficiency of the algorithm is greatly improved if they are newly calculated for each solution in which these parameters deviate from their reference values. A complete formulation of the estimates of the elasticities e_{ij} is provided in Tyers and Anderson 1992, Appendix 1. In practice, the criterion (31) is met after 3-10 iterations.

APPENDIX 2: SUPPLEMENTARY TABLES

Table 21— Exogenous growth in disposable income and agricultural productivity, Eastern Europe and the former Soviet Union, 1991-2010

Country Group/ Scenario/Period	Real Disposable Income	Productivity Growth in						
		Wheat	Coarse Grain	Rice	Ruminant Meat	Non-ruminant Meat	Dairy Products	Sugar
				(percent/year)				
EE-3								
Low-growth scenario								
Base-1991	−17.0	−2.0	−5.0	0.0	−10.0	−1.0	0.0	0.0
1991-92	−4.0	0.0	0.0	0.0	0.0	0.0	0.0	0.0
1992-93	4.0	2.0	3.0	2.0	2.5	3.0	2.5	1.0
1993-94	6.0	2.0	3.0	2.0	2.5	3.0	2.5	1.0
1994-95	8.0	2.0	3.0	2.0	2.5	3.0	2.5	1.0
1995-2010	4.0	2.0	3.0	2.0	2.5	3.0	2.5	1.0
High-growth scenario								
Base-1991	−8.0	−2.0	−5.0	0.0	−10.0	−1.0	0.0	0.0
1991-92	−2.0	0.0	0.0	0.0	0.0	0.0	0.0	0.0
1992-93	7.0	4.9	8.7	4.2	12.0	9.4	8.1	3.3
1993-94	9.0	4.9	8.7	4.2	12.0	9.4	8.1	3.3
1994-95	11.0	4.9	8.7	4.2	12.0	9.4	8.1	3.3
1995-2010	5.0	2.5	3.0	2.5	3.0	3.5	3.0	1.0
Balkans								
Low-growth scenario								
Base-1991	−32.0	−9.0	36.0	0.0	1.0	−2.0	0.0	0.0
1991-92	−18.0	−10.0	−25.0	0.0	−10.0	−10.0	−10.0	−10.0
1992-93	−10.0	0.0	0.0	0.0	0.0	0.0	0.0	0.0
1993-94	0.0	2.0	3.0	2.0	2.5	3.0	2.5	1.0
1994-95	4.0	2.0	3.0	2.0	2.5	3.0	2.5	1.0
1995-2010	3.0	2.0	3.0	2.0	2.5	3.0	2.5	1.0
High-growth scenario								
Base-1991	−16.0	−9.0	36.0	0.0	1.0	−2.0	0.0	0.0
1991-92	−9.0	−10.0	−25.0	0.0	−10.0	−10.0	−10.0	−10.0
1992-93	−5.0	2.0	3.0	2.0	2.5	3.0	2.5	1.0
1993-94	2.0	3.9	3.6	2.8	4.5	5.2	4.6	2.0
1994-95	6.0	3.9	3.6	2.8	4.5	5.2	4.6	2.0
1995-2010	5.0	3.9	3.6	2.8	4.5	5.2	4.6	2.0
Russia								
Low-growth scenario								
Base-1991	−9.0	−14.0	−14.0	. . .	−9.0	−9.0	−6.0	−21.0
1991-92	−19.0	10.0	10.0	. . .	−8.0	−8.0	−7.0	−10.0
1992-93	−12.0	1.0	1.0	. . .	2.5	3.0	2.5	1.0
1993-94	−4.0	1.0	1.0	. . .	2.5	3.0	2.5	1.0
1994-95	0.0	1.0	1.0	. . .	2.5	3.0	2.5	1.0
1995-2010	4.0	2.0	2.0	. . .	2.5	3.0	2.5	1.0
High-growth scenario								
Base-1991	−5.0	−14.0	−14.0	. . .	−9.0	−9.0	−6.0	−21.0
1991-92	−10.0	10.0	10.0	. . .	−8.0	−8.0	−7.0	−10.0
1992-93	−6.0	1.0	1.0	. . .	2.5	3.0	2.5	1.0
1993-94	2.0	2.6	2.3	. . .	5.0	5.6	6.1	3.5
1994-95	6.0	2.6	2.3	. . .	5.0	5.6	6.1	3.5
1995-2010	5.0	3.6	3.3	. . .	5.0	5.6	6.1	3.5
Ukraine								

(continued)

Table 21—Continued

Country Group/ Scenario/Period	Real Disposable Income	Wheat	Coarse Grain	Rice	Ruminant Meat	Non-ruminant Meat	Dairy Products	Sugar
					(percent/year)			
Low-growth scenario								
Base-1991	−13.0	−14.0	−14.0	...	−6.0	−6.0	−7.0	−21.0
1991-92	−15.0	8.0	8.0	...	−7.0	−7.0	−8.0	−10.0
1992-93	−10.0	1.0	1.0	...	2.5	3.0	2.5	2.0
1993-94	−2.0	1.0	1.0	...	2.5	3.0	2.5	2.0
1994-95	2.0	1.0	1.0	...	2.5	3.0	2.5	2.0
1995-2010	4.0	2.0	2.0	...	2.5	3.0	2.5	2.0
High-growth scenario								
Base-1991	−7.0	−14.0	−14.0	...	−6.0	−6.0	−7.0	−21.0
1991-92	−8.0	8.0	8.0	...	−7.0	−7.0	−8.0	−10.0
1992-93	−5.0	1.0	1.0	...	2.5	3.0	2.5	1.0
1993-94	2.0	2.6	2.3	...	4.7	5.3	6.3	3.5
1994-95	6.0	2.6	2.3	...	4.7	5.3	6.3	3.5
1995-2010	5.0	3.6	3.3	...	4.7	5.3	6.3	3.5
Baltics								
Low-growth scenario								
Base-1991	−14.0	0.0	0.0	...	−6.0	−6.0	−8.0	−21.0
1991-92	−34.0	0.0	0.0	...	−7.0	−7.0	−9.0	2.0
1992-93	−8.0	1.0	1.0	...	2.5	3.0	2.5	2.0
1993-94	−1.0	1.0	1.0	...	2.5	3.0	2.5	2.0
1994-95	2.0	1.0	1.0	...	2.5	3.0	2.5	2.0
1995-2010	4.0	2.0	2.0	...	2.5	3.0	2.5	2.0
High-growth scenario								
Base-1991	−7.0	0.0	0.0	...	−6.0	−6.0	−8.0	−21.0
1991-92	−17.0	0.0	0.0	...	−7.0	−7.0	−9.0	−10.0
1992-93	−4.0	1.5	2.7	...	10.9	11.4	14.7	11.8
1993-94	2.0	1.5	2.7	...	10.9	11.4	14.7	11.8
1994-95	6.0	1.5	2.7	...	10.9	11.4	14.7	11.8
1995-2010	5.0	2.5	2.0	...	3.0	4.0	4.0	1.5
Western Republics								
Low-growth scenario								
Base-1991	−15.0	0.0	0.0	...	−7.0	−7.0	−8.0	−21.0
1991-92	−22.0	0.0	0.0	...	−8.0	−8.0	−9.0	−10.0
1992-93	−14.0	1.0	1.0	...	2.5	3.0	2.5	1.0
1993-94	−6.0	1.0	1.0	...	2.5	3.0	2.5	1.0
1994-95	−1.0	1.0	1.0	...	2.5	3.0	2.5	1.0
1995-2010	3.0	2.0	2.0	...	2.5	3.0	2.5	1.0
High-growth scenario								
Base-1991	−8.0	0.0	0.0	...	−7.0	−7.0	−8.0	−21.0
1991-92	−11.0	0.0	0.0	...	−8.0	−8.0	−9.0	−10.0
1992-93	−7.0	1.0	1.0	...	2.5	3.0	2.5	1.0
1993-94	−1.0	1.8	1.7	...	4.9	5.4	6.4	3.5
1994-95	4.0	1.8	1.7	...	4.9	5.4	6.4	3.5
1995-2010	3.0	2.8	2.7	...	4.9	5.4	6.4	3.5
Kazakhstan								
Low-growth scenario								
Base-1991	−12.0	−38.0	−38.0	−38.0	0.0	0.0	−3.0	−21.0
1991-92	−14.0	20.0	20.0	35.0	0.0	0.0	−4.0	−10.0
1992-93	−12.0	1.0	1.0	2.0	2.5	3.0	2.5	1.0
1993-94	−5.0	1.0	1.0	2.0	2.5	3.0	2.5	1.0
1994-95	0.0	1.0	1.0	2.0	2.5	3.0	2.5	1.0
1995-2010	3.0	2.0	2.0	2.0	2.5	3.0	2.5	1.0
High-growth scenario								

(continued)

Table 21—Continued

Country Group/ Scenario/Period	Real Disposable Income	Wheat	Coarse Grain	Rice	Ruminant Meat	Non-ruminant Meat	Dairy Products	Sugar
					(percent/year)			
Base-1991	−6.0	−38.0	−38.0	−38.0	0.0	0.0	−3.0	−21.0
1991-92	−7.0	20.0	20.0	20.0	0.0	0.0	−4.0	−10.0
1992-93	−6.0	1.0	1.0	2.0	2.5	3.0	2.5	1.0
1993-94	0.0	5.1	5.0	6.1	3.9	4.5	5.7	3.5
1994-95	4.0	5.1	5.0	6.1	3.9	4.5	5.7	3.5
1995-2010	3.0	6.1	6.0	6.1	3.9	4.5	5.7	3.5
Central Asian Republics								
Low-growth scenario								
Base-1991	−2.0	0.0	0.0	0.0	−5.0	−5.0	0.0	−21.0
1991-92	−13.0	0.0	0.0	0.0	−5.0	−5.0	0.0	−21.0
1992-93	−5.0	1.0	1.0	2.0	2.5	3.0	2.5	1.0
1993-94	0.0	1.0	1.0	2.0	2.5	3.0	2.5	1.0
1994-95	2.0	1.0	1.0	2.0	2.5	3.0	2.5	1.0
1995-2010	3.0	2.0	2.0	2.0	2.5	3.0	2.5	1.0
High-growth scenario								
Base-1991	−1.0	0.0	0.0	0.0	−5.0	−5.0	0.0	−21.0
1991-92	−7.0	0.0	0.0	0.0	−5.0	−5.0	0.0	−21.0
1992-93	−2.0	1.0	1.0	2.0	2.5	3.0	2.5	1.0
1993-94	2.0	1.8	1.7	2.8	4.5	5.1	5.3	3.5
1994-95	4.0	1.8	1.7	2.8	4.5	5.1	5.3	3.5
1995-2010	3.0	2.8	2.7	2.8	4.5	5.1	5.3	3.5

Sources: The growth in real disposable income through 1992 is based on GDP growth estimates from International Monetary Fund, *World Economic Outlook* (Washington, D.C.: IMF, 1992). Thereafter, the two scenarios differ. The low-growth scenario has some intermediate recovery followed by the resumption of real growth at historical rates. The high-growth scenario has rapid catch-up over 1992-95, settling to slightly faster-than-trend growth in EE-3 and the Baltic states, and catch-up to the historical trend over the long haul from 1993 through 2010 elsewhere.

Productivity shifts in the interval base to 1991 and 1992 reflect recorded production shocks in each region. See S. S. Sheffield, "1991 Agricultural Performance in the Former USSR," *Economies in Transition Agriculture Report* 5 (January-February 1992): 2-6; and USDA (U.S. Department of Agriculture), Economic Research Service, "Central Europe: Agriculture in the New Market Economies," Special reprint from *Agricultural Outlook*, February 1992; USDA (U.S. Department of Agriculture), Economic Research Service, *Former USSR: Agriculture and Trade Report*, RS-92-1 Situation and Outlook Series (Washington, D.C.: USDA, 1992). Thereafter, the two scenarios differ. The low-growth scenario has the resumption of trend productivity growth in the region, while the high-growth scenario adds gains that are possible from the adoption of Western production techniques. Their levels and application are explained in the text.

Notes: Food price subsidies in the former Soviet Union are removed over the first five years in both scenarios. In J. Morduch, K. Brooks, and Y. M. Urinson, "Distributional Consequences of the Russian Price Liberalization," *Economic Development and Cultural Change* 4 (3, 1994), this is assumed to have substantially reduced average food purchasing power. In a previous analysis, purchasing power is reduced by a cumulative 18 percent (see R. Tyers, "Agricultural Sector Impacts of Economic Reform in Europe and the Former Soviet Union," *Journal of Economic Integration* 8 (2): 245-277). More recent information suggests the declines in observed consumption are too small to justify this assumption. Here, no such allowance is made and, as explained in the text, the subsidies are assumed to have been largely wasted in queuing and other allocative inefficiencies.

Table 22—Incremental effects of economic change combined with food price reform in the Balkans and the former Soviet Union, 2000

Effect	Rice	Wheat	Coarse Grain	Sugar	Dairy Products	Ruminant Meat	Non-ruminant Meat
				(percent)			
Effect on world prices							
Low-growth[a]	−11	−20	−16	−1	−3	−10	−4
High-growth[a]	−12	−23	−16	−2	−10	−10	−4
Change in consumption							
Balkans							
Low-growth	1	1	21	−23	−8	−16	−16
High-growth	14	4	16	−16	12	6	−3
Russia							
Low-growth	−39	−18	−12	−2	−20	−34	3
High-growth	−31	−14	−5	1	−8	−21	19
Ukraine							
Low-growth	−20	−21	−14	−5	−19	−33	4
High-growth	−12	−18	−8	2	−9	−21	19
Baltics							
Low-growth	−28	−42	−30	−17	−24	−39	−4
High-growth	−18	11	37	−2	−11	−25	14
Western republics							
Low-growth	−32	−25	−12	−4	−24	−40	−10
High-growth	−24	−20	−7	−0	−14	−28	8
Kazakhstan							
Low-growth	−22	−21	9	−1	−21	−32	3
High-growth	−18	−16	14	5	−10	−21	19
Central Asia							
Low-growth	−22	−17	0	4	−12	−22	18
High-growth	−19	−15	4	11	−6	−17	26
Change in production							
Balkans							
Low-growth	9	−6	32	4	1	11	24
High-growth	18	9	40	13	18	32	49
Russia							
Low-growth	...	14	14	−26	−16	−10	−10
High-growth	...	27	24	−12	6	7	8
Ukraine							
Low-growth	...	22	12	−19	−24	−11	−6
High-growth	...	34	21	−11	−3	3	10
Baltics							
Low-growth	...	24	15	−18	−22	−10	−5
High-growth	...	28	21	7	18	17	25
Western republics							
Low-growth	...	25	15	−25	−24	−11	−6
High-growth	...	31	20	−11	−4	4	11
Kazakhstan							
Low-growth	−19	6	−7	−27	−18	1	7
High-growth	7	38	24	−13	2	11	19
Central Asia							
Low-growth	−12	26	26	0	−12	−9	−5
High-growth	−8	28	18	0	6	5	11

(continued)

71

Table 22—Continued

Effect	Rice	Wheat	Coarse Grain	Sugar	Dairy Products	Ruminant Meat	Non-ruminant Meat
				(million metric tons)			
Change in net exports:[b]							
Balkans							
Low-growth	0.0	−1.3	3.9	0.4	1.1	0.3	1.2
High-growth	0.0	−0.8	7.7	0.4	0.7	0.3	1.6
Russia							
Low-growth	0.4	16.8	15.1	−0.7	3.4	1.5	−0.6
High-growth	0.3	21.4	16.4	−0.5	8.2	1.4	−0.7
Ukraine							
Low-growth	0.1	10.2	6.5	−0.8	−1.9	−0.4	−0.2
High-growth	0.0	12.3	7.7	−0.6	1.0	0.4	−0.1
Baltics							
Low-growth	0.0	1.7	1.3	0.1	−0.6	0.1	0.0
High-growth	0.0	0.5	−0.4	0.0	1.6	0.2	0.1
Western republics							
Low-growth	0.1	4.9	2.9	−0.1	0.2	0.3	0.0
High-growth	0.1	4.5	2.4	−0.1	1.3	0.3	0.0
Kazakhstan							
Low-growth	−0.2	2.1	−1.5	0.0	0.2	0.2	0.0
High-growth	0.1	5.5	1.8	−0.1	0.7	0.2	0.0
Central Asia							
Low-growth	0.0	3.5	0.5	0.0	0.4	0.1	−0.1
High-growth	0.0	3.0	−0.3	−0.1	0.7	0.1	−0.1

Source: Results from the analysis using the model described in Appendix 1.
Notes: These results examine the incremental effects of food market liberalization in the Balkans and the former Soviet Union. The reference simulation in this case includes unilateral EU reform and expansion of the European Union to include the European Free Trade Association countries, as well as extension of the CAP to cover EE-3 farmers (those in the former Czechoslovakia, Hungary, and Poland).
[a]The low- and high-growth scenarios here refer to the EE-3 (in the reference simulation used), the Balkans, and the former Soviet Union.
[b]Where positive, a change in net exports indicates increased exports or a reduction in net imports, depending on which prevailed in the reference case.

72

BIBLIOGRAPHY

Anderson, K. 1987. On why agriculture declines with economic growth. *Agricultural Economics* 1(3) (June): 195-207.

———. 1992. Will Eastern Europe and the Soviet Republics become major agricultural exporters? In *Improving agricultural trade performance under the GATT*, ed. T. Becker, R. Gray, and A. Schmitz, 5-27. Kiel: Vauk-Verlag.

———. 1993. Intersectoral changes in transforming socialist economies: Distinguishing initial from longer term responses. In *Economic growth and agriculture*, ed. I. Goldin, 291-321. London: Macmillan for the Organization for Economic Cooperation and Development.

Anderson, K., and R. Tyers. 1993. More on welfare gains to developing countries from liberalizing world food trade. *Journal of Agricultural Economics* 44 (May): 189-204.

———. 1994. Implications of EC expansion for European agricultural policies, trade and welfare. In *Expanding European regionalism: The EC's new members*, ed. R. Baldwin, P. Haaparanta, and J. Kiander. Cambridge: Cambridge University Press.

Andrews, N. P., and I. M. Roberts. 1992. *The Dunkel Uruguay Round text: Implications for agriculture—an Australian view.* Conference Paper 92.21. Canberra: Australian Bureau of Agricultural and Resource Economics.

Aslund, A. 1991. *Gorbachev's struggle for economic reform.* Ithaca, N.Y., U.S.A.: Cornell University Press.

———. 1992. Prospects for economic reform in the USSR. *World Bank Economic Review*, Proceedings Supplement (March): 43-70.

Atkin, M. 1992. *The international grain trade.* Cambridge, U.K.: Woodhead.

Balassa, B. 1990. *Perestroika and its implications for European socialist countries.* Working Paper Series No. 428. Washington, D.C.: World Bank.

Barro, R. J., and H. I. Grossman. 1974. Suppressed inflation and the supply multiplier. *Review of Economic Studies* 41 (January): 87-104.

Bautista, R. 1987. *Production incentives in Philippine agriculture: Effects of trade and exchange rate policies.* Research Report 59. Washington D.C.: International Food Policy Research Institute.

Beck, A. 1991. *Impact of economic upheavals in Eastern Europe and the Soviet Union on Australian minerals and energy markets.* Conference Paper 91.46. Canberra: Australian Bureau of Agricultural and Resource Economics.

Becker, G. S. 1965. A theory of the allocation of time. *Economic Journal* 299 (September): 493-517.

Bergson, A. 1991. The USSR before the fall: How poor and why? *Journal of Economic Perspectives* 5 (4): 29-44.

Blanchard, O., R. Dornbusch, P. Krugman, R. Layard, and L. Summers. 1991. *Reform in Eastern Europe*. Cambridge Mass., U.S.A.: MIT Press.

Borensztein, E. 1993. *The strategy of reform in the centrally planned economies of Eastern Europe: Lessons and challenges*. Papers on Policy Analysis and Assessment. Washington, D.C.: International Monetary Fund.

Boycko, M. 1992. When higher incomes reduce welfare: Queues, labor supply, and macro equilibrium in socialist economies. *Quarterly Journal of Economics* 107 (August): 907-920.

Brooks, K. 1991. Price adjustment and land valuation in the Soviet agricultural reform: A view using Lithuanian farm data. *European Review of Agricultural Economics* 18 (1): 19-36.

_____. 1993. Challenges of trade and agricultural development for East/Central Europe and the states of the former USSR. *Agricultural Economics* 8 (June): 401-420.

Brooks, K., and Z. Lerman. 1993. *Land reform and farm restructuring in Russia: 1992 status*. Washington, D.C.: World Bank.

Brooks, K., J. L. Guarsch, A. Braverman, and C. Csaki. 1991. Agriculture and the transition to the market. *Journal of Economic Perspectives* 5 (4): 149-161.

Burniaux, J.-M., and D. van der Mensbrugge. 1990. *The RUNS model: A rural-urban North-South general equilibrium model for agricultural policy analysis*. Technical Paper No. 33. Paris: Organization for Economic Cooperation and Development.

Camdessus, M. 1992. Economic transformation in the fifteen republics of the former USSR: A challenge or an opportunity for the world? Address to Georgetown University School of Foreign Service, April 15, as reported in *IMF Survey*, April 27, 131-134.

CARD (Centre for Agricultural and Rural Development). 1992a. *An analysis of the EC Commission plan for CAP reform*. GATT Research Paper 92-GATT-4. Ames, Iowa, U.S.A.: Iowa State University.

_____. 1992b. *Implications of a GATT agreement for world commodity markets, 1993-98: An analysis of the Dunkel text on agriculture*. GATT Research Paper 93-GATT-1. Ames, Iowa, U.S.A.: Iowa State University.

CEPR (Centre for Economic Policy Research). 1990. *Monitoring European integration: The impact of Eastern Europe*. Annual report. London: CEPR.

_____. 1992. *Monitoring European integration 3: Is bigger better? The economics of EC enlargement*. Annual report. London: CEPR.

Charemza, W. 1990. Parallel markets, excess demand and virtual prices: An empirical approach. *European Economic Review* 34 (May): 331-339.

Claasen, E.-M. 1991. Exchange rate policies in developing and post-socialist countries: An overview. In *Exchange rate policies in developing and post-socialist countries*, ed. E.-M. Claasen, chap.1. San Francisco: International Center for Economic Growth.

Cochrane, N. 1988. The private sector in East European agriculture. *Problems of Communism* 37 (March-April): 47-53.

Collins, S., and D. Rodrik. 1991. *Eastern Europe and the Soviet Union in the world economy*. Policy Analyses in International Economics No. 32. Washington, D.C.: Institute for International Economics.

Commission of the European Communities. 1991. The development and future of the Common Agricultural Policy. Communication of the Commission to the Council and to the European Parliament, Brussels, July.

Cook, E. 1988. *The Soviet livestock sector: Performance and prospects*. Foreign Agricultural Economic Report No. 235. Washington, D.C.: Economic Research Service, U.S. Department of Agriculture.

Cook, E., W. M. Liefert, and R. Koopman. 1991. *Government intervention in Soviet agriculture: Estimates of consumer and producer subsidy equivalents*. Staff Report No. AGES 9146. Washington, D.C.: U.S. Department of Agriculture, Economic Research Service.

Corden, W. M. 1984. Booming sector and Dutch disease economics: Survey and consolidation. *Oxford Economic Papers* 36 (November): 359-380.

_____. 1992. *Trade policy and exchange rate issues in the former Soviet Union*. Working Paper Series No. 915. Washington, D.C.: World Bank.

Coricelli, F., and R. de R. Rocha. 1991. Stabilization programs in Eastern Europe: A comparative analysis of the Polish and Yugoslav programs of 1990. In *Reforming Central and Eastern European economies: Initial results and challenges*, ed. V. Corbo, F. Coricelli, and J. Bossak, 101-134. Washington, D.C.: World Bank.

Csaki, C. 1992. *Transformation of agriculture in Central Eastern Europe and the former USSR: Major policy issues and perspectives*. Working Paper Series No. 888. Washington, D.C.: World Bank.

Desai, P. 1986. *Weather and grain yields in the Soviet Union*. Research Report 54. Washington D.C.: International Food Policy Research Institute.

Devarajan, S., J. D. Lewis, and S. Robinson. 1993. External shocks, purchasing power parity and the equilibrium real exchange rate. *World Bank Economic Review* 7 (January): 45-63.

Dorosh, P., and A. Valdés. 1990. *Effects of exchange rate and trade policies on agriculture in Pakistan*. Research Report 84. Washington D.C.: International Food Policy Research Institute.

Economist. 1993a. Ruble millionaires. October, 58.

_____. 1993b. The Yeltsinisation of Russia. November, 49.

Erzan, R., C. Holmes, and R. Safadi. 1992. *How changes in the former CMEA area may affect international trade in manufactures*. Working Paper Series No. 973. Washington, D.C.: World Bank.

Euroconsult. 1991. Survey on pricing policy and food distribution in the USSR/RSFSR. A report prepared for the European Bank for Reconstruction and Development, London.

Fane, G. 1991. The social opportunity cost of foreign exchange: A partial defence of Harberger el al. *The Economic Record*, December: 307-316.

_____. 1992. The average and marginal domestic resource costs of foreign exchange. Research School of Pacific Studies, Australian National University.

FAO (Food and Agriculture Organization of the United Nations). Various years. Food Balance Sheet Tape. Rome.

Folmer, C., M. A. Keyzer, M. D. Merbis, H. J. J. Stowijk, and P. J. J. Veenendaal. 1993. CAP reform and its differential impact on member states. Staff Working Paper WP-92-02R. Centre for World Food Studies, Amsterdam.

Galbraith, J. K. 1992. *The culture of contentment*. London: Sinclair-Stevenson.

Gardner, B., and K. Brooks. 1994. Marketing and food prices in Russia after price liberalization. Paper presented at the annual conference of the Allied Social Science Associations, Boston, January 3-5.

GATT (General Agreement on Tariffs and Trade). 1991. Draft final act embodying the results of the Uruguay Round of multilateral trade negotiations. Trade Negotiations Committee, GATT Secretariat, Geneva.

_____. 1994. *Uruguay Round Protocol to the General Agreement on Tariffs and Trade 1994*. Geneva.

Gelb, A., and C. W. Gray. 1991. *The transformation of economies in Central and Eastern Europe: Issues, progress, and prospects*. Policy and Research Series 17. Washington, D.C.: World Bank.

Gray, K. R., and S. Sheffield. 1992. Food consumption in the former USSR and its republics 1980-1991. *Economies in Transition Report* 5 (March/April): 1-14.

Haley, S. L., M. T. Herlihy, and B. Johnson. 1991. Estimating trade liberalization effects for U.S. grains and cotton. *Review of Agricultural Economics* 13(1): 19-43.

Hamilton, C. B. and L. A. Winters. 1992a. *Opening up international trade in Eastern Europe*. Seminar Paper No. 511. Stockholm: Institute for International Economic Studies, Stockholm University.

_____. 1992b. Trade with Eastern Europe. *Economic Policy* 14 (April): 78-116.

Havrylyshyn, O., and J. Williamson. 1991. *From Soviet disUnion to Eastern Economic Community?* Policy Analyses in International Economics No.35. Washington, D.C.: Institute for International Economics.

Hertel, T. W. 1989. PSEs and the mix of measures to support farm incomes. *The World Economy* 12 (1): 17-28.

Hinojosa-Ojeda, R., S. Robinson, and J. Tesche. 1992. *Hungary, Austria and the European Community: A CGE model of economic reform and integration.* Washington D.C.: World Bank.

IMF (International Monetary Fund). 1992a. *International financial statistics.* Washington, D.C., September.

_____. 1992b. *The Russian Federation.* Economic Review Series, Washington D.C.: IMF.

_____. 1992c. *World economic outlook.* Washington D.C.: IMF.

_____. 1993. *World economic outlook.* Washington, D.C.: IMF.

IMF (International Monetary Fund), World Bank, Organization for Economic Cooperation and Development, and European Bank for Reconstruction and Development. 1991. *A study of the Soviet economy.* 3 vols. Paris: OECD.

Johnson, D. G. 1975. World agriculture, commodity policy and price variability. *American Journal of Agricultural Economics* 57 (December): 823-828.

_____. 1990. Possible impacts of agricultural trade liberalization on the USSR. *Comparative Economic Studies* 32 (2): 144-154.

_____. 1992. *World agriculture in disarray,* 2nd ed. London: Macmillan for the Trade Policy Research Centre.

Johnson, S. R., and A. A. Nikonov. 1991. Soviet agrarian reform and the food crisis: Neither can be ignored. *Choices* (Fourth Quarter): 7-11.

Josling, T. E. 1973. *Agricultural protection: Domestic policy and international trade.* C73/LIM/9, Rome: FAO.

Josling, T. E., and S. Tangermann. 1992. *MacSharry or Dunkel: Which plan reforms the CAP?* Lisbon: Instituto Superior de Agronomía.

Karp, L., and S. Stefanou. 1992. *Polish agriculture in transition: Does it hurt to be slapped by an invisible hand?* Discussion Paper No. 622. London: Centre for Economic Policy Research.

Konovalov, V., D. Tarr, J. Rhee, A. Kireyev, S. Stankovski, and L. Goldberg. 1993. *Russia: Joining the world economy.* Washington, D.C.: World Bank.

Koopman, R. B. 1989. *Efficiency and growth in agriculture: A comparative study of the Soviet Union, United States, Canada and Finland.* Staff Report No. AGES 89-54. Washington, D.C.: U.S. Department of Agriculture, Economic Research Service.

_____. 1992. Agriculture's role during the transition from plan to market: Real prices, real incentives and potential equilibrium. Paper prepared for a conference on Economic Statistics for the Economies in Transition: Eastern Europe in the 1990s, Economic Research Service, U.S. Department of Agriculture, Washington D.C.

Krueger, A. O., M. Schiff, and A. Valdés. 1988. Agricultural incentives in developing countries: Measuring the impact of sector-specific and economy-wide policies on agricultural incentives in LDCs. *World Bank Economic Review* (September): 255-272.

Kumi, A. 1992. An assessment of the likely impact of the liberalization of the Soviet economy on Soviet patterns of trade. Ph.D. diss., Iowa State University, Ames, Iowa, U.S.A..

Laird, S., and A. J. Yeats. 1992. The magnitude of two sources of bias in standard partial equilibrium trade simulation models. *Journal of Policy Modeling* 14 (1): 121-130.

Liefert, W. M. 1988. The full cost of Soviet oil and natural gas production. *Comparative Economic Studies* 30 (2): 1-20.

_____. 1990. The Soviet gain from trade with the West in fuel, grain and machinery. *Weltwirtschaftliches Archiv* 126 (1): 78-96.

_____. 1991. An elasticities approach to estimating excess demand in price-controlled markets. Economic Research Service, U.S. Department of Agriculture, Washington, D.C.

_____. 1992. Distribution problems in the food economy. In *The economies of the republics of the former USSR*. Washington, D.C.: Joint Economic Committee of the U.S. Congress.

Liefert, W. M., E. Cook, and R. Koopman. 1989. *World agricultural trade liberalization and the USSR*. Washington, D.C.: U.S. Department of Agriculture, Economic Research Service.

Liefert, W. M., R. B. Koopman, and E. C. Cook. 1991. *The effect of Soviet agricultural trade liberalization on the USSR*. Washington, D.C.: U.S. Department of Agriculture, Economic Research Service.

Lundell, M. R. 1992. Developments in Central and East European agricultural trade. U.S. Department of Agriculture, Economic Research Service, Washington D.C.

MacMillan, J., J. Whalley, and L. Zhu. 1989. The impact of China's economic reforms on agricultural productivity growth. *Journal of Political Economy* 97 (August): 781-807.

McAuley, A. 1979. *Economic welfare in the Soviet Union*. Madison, Wisc., U.S.A.: University of Wisconsin Press.

McKibbin, W. J. 1991. *The new Europe and its economic implications for the world economy*. Brookings Discussion Papers in International Economics 89. Washington, D.C.: The Brookings Institution.

McKibbin, W. J., and J. D. Sachs. 1991. *Global linkages: Macroeconomic interdependence and cooperation in the world economy*. Washington D.C.: The Brookings Institution.

McKinnon, R. I. 1991. Stabilizing the ruble: The problem of internal currency convertability. In *Exchange rate policies in developing and post-socialist countries*, ed. E.-M. Claasen, chap. 3. San Francisco: International Centre for Economic Growth.

Messerlin, P. A. 1992a. *The association agreements between the EC and Central Europe: Trade liberalization vs constitutional failure?* Paris: Institut d'Etudes Politiques de Paris.

————. 1992b. *The trade relations between the European Community and the Central and Eastern European countries.* Paris: Institut d'Etudes Politiques de Paris.

Michalopoulos, C., and D. Tarr. 1992. *Trade and payments arrangements for states of the former USSR.* Studies of Economies in Transformation Paper No. 2. Washington, D.C.: World Bank.

Morduch, J., K. Brooks, and Y. M. Urinson. 1994. Distributional consequences of the Russian price liberalization. *Economic Development and Cultural Change* 4(3): 469-483.

Moskoff, W. 1984. *Labor and leisure in the Soviet Union.* New York: St. Martin's Press.

Murphy, K. M., A. Shleifer and R. W. Vishny. 1992. The transition to a market economy: Pitfalls of partial reform. *Quarterly Journal of Economics* (August): 889-906.

Murrell, P. 1991a. Symposium on economic transition in the Soviet Union and Eastern Europe. *Journal of Economic Perspectives* 5 (4): 3-10.

————. 1991b. Can neoclassical economics underpin the reform of centrally-planned economies? *Journal of Economic Perspectives* 5 (4): 59-76.

Neary, J. P., and K. W. S. Roberts. 1980. The theory of household behavior under rationing. *European Economic Review* 13:25-42.

Nikonov, A. 1992. *Transition period in agriculture of Russia and other states of ex-union of the SSR.* Moscow: Agrarian Institute of the Russian Academy of Agricultural Sciences.

Nordhaus, W. D. 1990. Soviet economic reform: The longest road. *Brookings Papers on Economic Activity* 1: 287-318.

OECD (Organisation for Economic Cooperation and Development). 1990. *Modelling the effects of agricultural policies.* Economic Studies No.13. Paris.

————. 1991. *The Soviet agro-food system and agricultural trade: Prospects for reform.* Paris: OECD, Committee for Agriculture.

————. 1992. *Agricultural policies, markets and trade: Monitoring and outlook 1992.* Paris.

Overbosch, G., and W. Tims. 1992. Possible implications of reform in Eastern Europe and the ex-USSR for the food situation in developing countries. Research Memorandum 92-01, Centre for World Food Studies, Amsterdam. Mimeo.

Paarlberg, P. L. 1992. *The evolving farm structure in Eastern Germany.* Working Paper No. 92-9. International Agricultural Trade Research Consortium. West Lafayette, Ind., U.S.A.: Purdue University.

Parikh, K. S., G. Fischer, K. Frohberg, and O. Gulbrandsen. 1988. *Towards free trade in agriculture*. Amsterdam: Mortimers Nijhoff for the International Institute for Applied Systems Analysis.

Penn, J. B. 1989. Poland's food situation. *Choices* (Fourth Quarter): 3-7.

PlanEcon. 1992. *Currency report* 8 (4, 5, 6): 10-13.

Rodrik, D. 1992. *Making sense of the Soviet trade shock in Eastern Europe: A framework and some estimates*. Working Paper 4112. Cambridge, Mass., U.S.A.: National Bureau of Economic Research.

Roemer, M., and S. C. Radelet. 1991. Macroeconomic reform in developing countries. In *Reforming economic systems in developing countries*, ed. D. H. Perkins and M. Roemer, chap. 2. Cambridge, Mass., U.S.A.: Harvard University Press for the Harvard Institute for International Development.

Roningen, V. O. 1986. *A static world policy simulation (SWOPSIM) modelling framework*. Economic Research Service Staff Report No. AGES 860625. Washington, D.C.: U.S. Department of Agriculture.

Roningen, V. O., and P. M. Dixit. 1991. *Measuring agricultural trade distortion: A simple approach*. Economic Research Service. Staff Report No. AGES 9145. Washington, D.C.: U.S. Department of Agriculture.

Sah, R. K. 1987. Queues, rations and market: Comparisons of outcomes for the poor and the rich. *American Economic Review* 77 (March): 69-77.

Saxon, E., R. Tyers, and P. R. Phillips. 1992. *World agricultural production and trade: Price and quantity data*. Technical Paper No. 9. Canberra: International Economic Data Bank, Australian National University.

Schiff, M., and A. Valdés. 1992. *Synthesis: The economics of agricultural price interventions in developing countries*. Series on the Political Economy of Agricultural Pricing Policy, vol. 4. Baltimore, Md., U.S.A.: Johns Hopkins University Press.

Scott, H. G. 1992. *Liberalization and food security: A specific factor model*. Discussion Paper No. 92-8, Department of Economics. Birmingham, U.K.: University of Birmingham.

Sedik, D. J. 1992. Per capita GDP and meat consumption in the former USSR. *Economies in Transition Agriculture Report* 5 (July-August): 11-15.

Sheffield, S. S. 1992. 1991 agricultural performance in the former USSR. *Economies in Transition Agriculture Report* 5 (January-February): 2-6.

Shleifer, A., and R. Vishny. 1992. Pervasive shortages under socialism. *RAND Journal of Economics* 23 (2): 237-246.

Sicular, T. 1989. China: Food pricing under socialism. In *Food price policy in Asia: A comparative study*, ed. T. Sicular. Ithaca, N.Y., U.S.A.: Cornell University Press.

_____. 1991. China's agricultural policy during the reform period. In *Study papers submitted to the Joint Economic Committee of the U.S. Congress* 1 (April): 340-364.

Solimano, A. 1991. The economies of Central and Eastern Europe: An historical and international perspective. In *Reforming Central and Eastern European economies: Initial results and challenges*, ed. V. Corbo, F. Coricelli, and J. Bossak, chap. 7. Washington, D.C.: World Bank.

Sremac, D. 1992. Country profile and economic survey of the former Yugoslav republics. U.S. Department of Agriculture, Economic Research Service, Washington, D.C.

Stahl, D. O., and M. Alexeev. 1985. The influence of black markets on a queue-rationed centrally planned economy. *Journal of Economic Theory* 35: 234-250.

Sullivan, J., V. Roningen, S. Leetma, and D. Gray. 1992. *A 1989 global database for the static world policy simulation (SWOPSIM) modeling framework*. Economic Research Service, Staff Report No. AGES 9215. Washington, D.C.: U.S. Department of Agriculture.

Summers, R., and A. Heston. 1991. The Penn World Tables (Mark 5): An expanded set of international comparisons, 1950-1988. *Quarterly Journal of Economics* 106 (May): 327-368.

Swinnen, J. F. M. 1992. The development of price and trade policies in CEE agriculture: An endogenous policy theory perspective. Paper presented at the 31st European Seminar of the European Association of Agricultural Economists, Institute of Agricultural Economics, University of Frankfurt, Frankfurt, Germany, December.

Tangermann, S. 1993. Some economic effects of preferential trading agreements between the European Community and Central Europe. *Journal of Economic Integration* 8 (2): 152-174.

Tangermann, S., T. E. Josling, and S. Pearson. 1987. Multilateral negotiations on firm support levels. *The World Economy* 10 (3): 265-281.

Tarr, D. 1991. *When does rent-seeking augment the benefits of price and trade reform on rationed commodities?* Working Paper Series No. 741. Washington, D.C.: World Bank.

_____. 1992. *Terms of trade effects on countries of the former Soviet Union of moving to world prices*. Washington, D.C.: World Bank.

Tobin, J. 1975. A survey of the theory of rationing. In *Essays in economics*, vol. 2, ed. J. Tobin, 321-358. Amsterdam: North-Holland.

Tulpule, V., G. Tie, I. M. Roberts, A. Malarz, and J. Dlugosz. 1991. Changes in Eastern Europe and the Soviet Union: Prospects and challenges. *Agriculture and Resources Quarterly* 3 (March): 53-65.

Tyers, R. 1984. *Agricultural protection and market insulation: Analysis of international impacts by stochastic simulation.* Pacific Economic Papers No. 111. Canberra: Australia-Japan Research Centre, Australian National University.

———. 1991. On the neglect of dynamics, risk and market insulation in the analysis of Uruguay Round food trade reforms. *Australian Journal of Agricultural Economics* 35 (December): 295-313.

———. 1993. Agricultural sector impacts of economic reform in Europe and the former Soviet Union. *Journal of Economic Integration* 8 (2): 245-277.

———. 1994. Post Uruguay Round agricultural policy reform in the Asian "Big 4": Potential effects on the international terms of trade. Paper presented at the Grain in Developing Asia Workshop, Research School of Pacific Studies, Australian National University, Canberra, February 28.

Tyers, R., and K. Anderson. 1989. Price elasticities in international food trade: Synthetic estimates from a global model. *Journal of Policy Modeling* 11 (3): 315-344.

———. 1992. *Disarray in world food markets: A quantitative assessment.* Cambridge, U.K.: Cambridge University Press.

Tyers, R., and R. Falvey. 1989. Border price changes and domestic welfare in the presence of subsidized exports. *Oxford Economic Papers* 41: 434-451.

Urban, F. 1992. Levels and rates of growth of population in the FSU and Newly Independent States. *Economies in Transition Agriculture Report* 5 (March/April): 61.

USDA (U.S. Department of Agriculture), Economic Research Service. 1989. Poland restructures. *Agricultural outlook*, November.

———. 1992a. *Agricultural policies and performance in Central and Eastern Europe 1989-1992.* Washington D.C.: U.S. Department of Agriculture.

———. 1992b. Central Europe: Agriculture in the new market economies. Special reprint from *Agricultural Outlook*, February.

———. 1992c. *Former USSR: Agriculture and trade report.* RS-92-1 Situation and Outlook Series. Washington, D.C.: USDA.

Valdés, A. 1992a. *Gaining momentum: Economywide and agricultural reform in Latin America.* Washington, D.C.: World Bank.

———. 1992b. The macroeconomic and overall trade policy environment necessary to complement agricultural trade and price policy reforms. In *Agricultural policy reforms and regional market integration in Malawi, Zambia, and Zimbabwe*, ed. A. Valdés and K. Muir-Leresche, 11-31. Washington, D.C.: International Food Policy Research Institute.

Vanous, J. 1992. Prospects for economic reform in Eastern Europe. *World Bank Economic Review, Proceedings Supplement* (March): 71-82.

Webb, A. J., M. Lopez, and R. Penn. 1990. *Estimates of producer and consumer subsidy equivalents: Government intervention in agriculture, 1982-87.* Statistical Bulletin No. 803. Washington, D.C.: U.S. Department of Agriculture, Economic Research Service.

Weitzman, M. 1991. Price distortion and shortage deformation, or what happened to the soap? *American Economic Review* 81 (June): 401-414.

Williamson, J. 1991. *The opening of Eastern Europe.* Policy Analyses in International Economics No. 31. Washington, D.C.: Institute for International Economics.

World Bank. 1990. *World development report 1990.* New York: Oxford University Press.

_____. 1992a. *Measuring the incomes of economies of the former Soviet Union.* Working Paper Series No. 1057. Washington, D.C.

_____. 1992b. Review of food policy options and agricultural sector reforms. Joint report to the Russian Federation and members of the Commonwealth of Independent States, Washington D.C.

_____. 1992c. *The Russian Federation: Country economic memorandum,* 2 vols. Washington D.C.

_____. 1992d. *World development report 1992.* New York: Oxford University Press.

World Bank, International Monetary Fund, the Organization for Economic Cooperation and Development, and the European Bank for Reconstruction and Development. 1990. *The economy of the USSR.* Washington, D.C.: World Bank, OECD.

Zietz, J., and A. Valdés. 1988. *Agriculture in the GATT: An analysis of alternative approaches to reform.* Research Report 70. Washington D.C.: International Food Policy Research Institute.

Rod Tyers is a reader in economics in the Faculty of Economics and Commerce, Department of Economics, Australian National University at Canberra, Australia. He was a visiting research at IFPRI in 1992.